PERSONAL COMMITMENTS
Beginning, Keeping, Changing

REVISED EDITION

Margaret A. Farley

ORBIS BOOKS
Maryknoll, New York 10545

Founded in 1970, Orbis Books endeavors to publish works that enlighten the mind, nourish the spirit, and challenge the conscience. The publishing arm of the Maryknoll Fathers and Brothers, Orbis seeks to explore the global dimensions of the Christian faith and mission, to invite dialogue with diverse cultures and religious traditions, and to serve the cause of reconciliation and peace. The books published reflect the views of their authors and do not represent the official position of the Maryknoll Society. To learn more about Maryknoll and Orbis Books, please visit our website at http://www.maryknollsociety.org.

Library of Congress Cataloging-in-Publication Data

Farley, Margaret A.
    Personal commitments : beginning, keeping, changing / Margaret A. Farley.—Revised Edition.
        pages cm
    Includes bibliographical references and index.
    ISBN 978-1-62698-027-3 (pbk.)
    1. Commitment (Psychology)   2. Interpersonal relations.   3. Ethics.
I. Title.
BF619.F36 2013
177'.7—dc23

                                                                    2012045037

For my parents
John Arthur Farley and Mary Mosher Farley
with love and with honor

Contents

Preface

From the opening paragraphs of the first chapter to the closing paragraphs of the last, my concern to take seriously the experience of concrete individuals should be evident. I hope, however, that what I do in this book makes it clear that questions of personal commitment are also social questions, just as social problems are inevitably someone's personal problems. Social contexts shape our experiences of personal commitment; and without an understanding of these contexts, our understanding of personal commitments is limited. My focus on personal commitments represents my conviction that social analysis does not substitute for reflecting on the experience of individuals but that the two tasks are interrelated and both essential. Moreover, my moves from the descriptive to the normative represent my conviction that interpretation of our experience, as well as discernment for our decisions, requires clarity in moral concepts and moral reasoning.

This revised edition serves primarily to update developments in the socio-cultural milieu that provides the background for the analysis and argument of the book as a whole.

I was helped in writing the first edition of this book by many colleagues, friends, family members, students, and those with whom I have shared community. These included: Gilmary Bauer, Mary Rose D'Angelo, Leslie Griffin, Patricia Hammell, David Hollenbach, Gene Outka, Mary Valenti, and Catherine Vincie. Others whose support at that time was invaluable included my now deceased colleagues and friends Margaret Ann Baker, Gretchen Elliott, Emily George, Christopher Mooney, and Jules Toner. This revised edition became a possibility through the suggestion and urging of James M. Gustafson, and through the ready and wonderful support of Orbis Books, particularly editors Susan Perry and James Keane.

Chapter 1

Commitment and
Its Discontents

It was about forty years ago when I first became intrigued by the concept of commitment—its possibilities, significance, potential contradictions, and the wisdom or foolishness of its dismissal or embrace. This was in the 1970s, a time in Western culture when it was fashionable to call commitment into question, not just in its specific forms or in the concrete difficulties of individual or social relations, but—as many said—"in principle," in itself. This was the time when we were still reeling from the 1960s, from vast upheaval and loss of corporate faith, from new concern for "authenticity," yet creeping doubt and disillusionment regarding all forms of human affairs. On the one hand, it was a time for demythologizing human commitments; on the other, it marked a resurgent concern for commitment to values, persons, fundamental convictions, groups, and causes.

SOCIAL AND HISTORICAL TURBULENCE

All significant concepts, and all interpretations of concrete human experiences, take on meaning from the context in which they appear. If we go back to the beginning of the twentieth century (admittedly a short history, but a revealing one), it is not difficult to trace changing nuances in meanings and variations in appreciation of a concept like commitment. Larger social, political, cultural, and intellectual contexts surely shaped variations in understandings of human commitment, depending on, for example, whether the times were marked by war or peace, dominance of religious beliefs or moral and religious skepticism, reliance on or disappointment in major

1

institutions, rises and falls in economic security, the forcefulness
of new ideas, new forms of art and music, new developments in
technology. If we look back to an even shorter historical span—
to the 1950s, when whole populations considered commitments
to be "settled" and "taken for granted"—we find rumblings of
change already heard in critiques of "the organization man" and in
expressions of dissatisfaction with some frameworks of commitment.
Sightings even then of future globalization and new possibilities for
multicultural perspectives threatened to shake foundations of trust
and obligation built primarily on assumed universal human major
and minor commitments.

The resistance to conformity that began in the late 1950s reached
a kind of peak in the next decade with the rise of countercultures of
various sorts, and it continued into the early 1970s. Overall awareness
of rapid cultural change prompted startling recognitions of personal
changes within individual lives. Goals shifted from personal maturity,
responsibility, fidelity, to an overriding preoccupation with personal
growth, new experiences, and new relationships, self-actualization
beyond traditional boundaries. Traditional objects of commitments,
such as family, country, church, were challenged on the basis of new
interpretations of human experience. Totalistic, sometimes fanatic,
commitments were undertaken to various causes, but they often
ended in a sense of powerlessness and disappointment. All of these
developments helped to suggest the need for changing or abandoning
otherwise permanent commitments.

Some of the most relentless questions regarding commitment in
these years were raised by women, as their self-consciousness grew
amidst the concrete circumstances of their lives. At first, reflection on
their experience brought recognition of deep needs in the human
spirit for commitment, and realization of the bitter pain of desertion
or neglect in commitments that were thought to be mutual. As the
years went by, women's struggles evolved into the need to balance
multiple commitments, forestall guilt incurred in compromise or
change of commitments, and accept limitations without abandoning
trust or hope in a reasonable future. For women, in particular,
historical contexts shed light on both the limitations of and possibility
for commitments. Economic advantage or disadvantage, social

dependency, marginalization or new positions of power, culturally conditioned modes of self-esteem, society's racism: all shaped the structures of their commitments, for better or for worse. Instancing the importance of social factors, in this case racial factors, Audre Lorde insisted: "Some problems we [black or white] share as women, some we do not. You fear your children will grow up to join the patriarchy and testify against you, we fear our children will be dragged from a car and shot down in the street, and you will turn your backs upon the reasons they are dying."[1]

What might be called an epoch of social critique regarding commitments was chronicled and analyzed by sociologists and psychologists as a time of "the uncommitted." Observers like Kenneth Keniston told of a 1960s generation of young men who, "face to face with a multitude of opportunities," avoided them all and ended up resenting "the freedom that makes them responsible for their own fate."[2] A decade later, Margaret Mead wondered how a youthful generation that doubted the sufficient value of anything to justify commitment could continue to build a culture. She described the "suicide of the fortunate and the gifted" in the face of what they perceived to be an empty future.[3] And it was not only the young who fled commitment but the middle-aged and the old. Spouses could be changed, and jobs could be left behind. Religiously interpreted vocations could be transferred from one framework to another.

The overwhelming tendency to question the value of commitments as such, however, moderated to a great extent after the 1960s and 1970s. Sociological studies of the 1980s were more likely to *call* for commitment than to criticize it, and to lament failures to keep commitments. Reacting against certain kinds of individualism (blamed for idolizing forms of freedom that led to casual sex, alienation from community, and unbridled competition), social analysts actually proposed an "ethics of commitment,"[4] a "generosity of spirit in which you are willing to invest emotional commitment in other people and other things,"[5] a "common commitment to ourselves and future generations."[6]

Moreover, and somewhat ironically, all through the years from the 1960s to the early 1990s challenges to commitment were often accompanied not by wholesale indifference to values and loyalties, but by passionate alternative cries for greater commitment. What was decried was superficiality, rigidity, double standards, gendered stereotypes of commitments—attitudes and honored perspectives that many believed were fostered by uncritical and complacent adherence to established and ossified institutions and structures. Paradoxically, these years were marked by strong social movements that motivated profound commitments on the part of their followers. Whether women's movements, anti-war movements, anti-racist and anti-apartheid movements, environmental movements, gay and lesbian movements, and many others, all represented the antithesis of loss of concern for commitment. Their very processes as movements were sustained by the commitments of those at their core as well as on their peripheries. Within both the critiques of commitment, however, and the new concern for authentic commitments were the seeds for questioning traditional understandings of commitment.

In the twenty-first century, interest in the *concept* of commitment, whether social or interpersonal, may have waned. Rebellions might seem to be over (in the West), though they may remain just beneath the surface of new political movements such as "Tea Party" or "Occupy" movements. There is, of course, plenty of evidence that commitments sit somewhat lightly on people's agendas—as in statistics about changing membership commitments from one church to another, or to no church at all;[7] and as in the somewhat trivializing appeal to commitment that is found in popular journals and on-line self-help offerings.[8] But in fact few persons now question some general practical need for promise-making and contract-forming in the many realms of human life and activity. And even fewer challenge the concept of commitment as necessary and desirable in the central relationships and major undertakings of everyone's lives.

This said, it is difficult to detect just what is going on regarding individual and social commitments today. Take the highly visible realm of marriage and its frequent correlative, divorce. There are multiple statistical studies of these activities as well as multiple and nondefinitive interpretations of what the statistics really mean. Comparisons between the United States and Sweden are considered most interesting as harbingers of the future. For example, between 1980 and 2008 the number of marriages in the U.S. went from 15.9 to 10.6 (per 1,000 population aged 15 to 64 years); and in Sweden from 7.4 to 8.3.[9] The percentage of divorces in that same time and populations went from 7.9 to 5.2 in the U.S. and 3.7 to 3.5 in Sweden. In neither of these two countries do the bare statistics take into account cohabitation, second marriages after divorce, or even "registered partnerships" such as civil unions in the U.S. Nor do they take into account factors of age, level of education, economic status, or particular legislation regarding either marriage or divorce.[10] Interpreters puzzle over what these official marital trends mean. What form of commitment, for example, is involved in long-term cohabitation (such as occurs in Sweden) and shorter-term cohabitation (in the U.S. where it is largely preliminary to marriage, at least in original intention). What difference do diverse legal arrangements in these and other countries make to the reality of marriage and family commitments?[11] Does general tolerance of divorce make desires for lasting commitment stronger or less strong?

What is clear is that partnerships that are alternative to heterosexual marriage are much more accepted in Western societies than they were in the past, even the recent past. Despite ongoing "culture wars," cohabitation, single parenting, and same-sex unions or marriages are more and more accepted (and understood) in ways that point to new forms of commitment, not the rejection of commitment. Moreover, there is no general lack of respect for commitment regarding parenting and loyalty to family. Parenting may be delayed until later in persons' lives than was previously customary, but it is often thereby taken more seriously as a decision and a new level of commitment. Other examples of the waxing, not waning, of commitment as a concept and a practice can also be adduced, as in our acceptance of the idea that second and third careers can be both necessary and responsible choices for individual persons. Perhaps above all, we have learned that the destructiveness of one framework for commitment need not mean that all commitments are therefore useless or bad.

THEORETICAL CONSTRUCTIONS

From the late twentieth century on, each phase of Western social struggle over the meaning and value of commitment brought new theories to reinforce or remedy doubts about its viability. In 1970, at the height of skepticism about commitment, the psychiatrist Robert Jay Lifton articulated what became a famous profile of a new kind of person, one characterized by "self-process" rather than an integrated personality or character.[12] What Lifton called the new "protean man" (or woman) was like the ancient god Proteus, who continually changed his form so that he would not be recognized. Life for such a person was a series of relationships, tasks, occupations, ideologies—tentatively adopted like masks, tried like experiments, and let go of without inner struggle or regret.

The problem of commitment was analyzed both pre- and post-1970 not only by sociologists and psychologists but by philosophers. It was frequently argued that long-term commitments are simply not possible for human persons; or when they are possible, they are unwise. Commitment is impossible, so the argument went, because human freedom of choice simply does not have the power to control the future. The French philosopher Jean-Paul Sartre provided the example of a compulsive gambler who "commits" himself never to gamble again. The gambler does not thereby assure that he will not do so. When faced with another opportunity for gambling, suddenly his resolutions and promises fade away. He may turn to them, wanting not to gamble, thinking that his commitment should have some power to keep him from gambling. "The earlier resolution of 'not playing anymore' is always *there*, and . . . the gambler when in the presence of the gaming table, turns toward it [the resolution] as if to ask it for help."[13] But to no avail. The promise, the commitment, is inert; a whole new choice must be made.

The theoretical inefficacy of commitment appeared to prevail not only in relation to what we generally call addictions today. Its lack of power to affect our future seemed even more obvious to those who worried about the possibility of commitments to love someone. Love, it was frequently maintained, is not the sort of thing that can be bound, obligated. No one can predict if a love will endure. If anyone tries to promise it forever, they inevitably find themselves having to pretend that their feelings have not changed. Someday, they will be dishonest to the one they love today; or at the very least they will have to deceive themselves about their modified love.

Philosophers observed that even on a small scale we have experience of our desires changing, so that what we commit ourselves to at one moment leads to hypocrisy at another. The promise I make to a friend that I will visit her in the hospital every day all too easily degenerates into sheer duty for me and a kind of sham for my friend. These philosophers were only saying what others, like the nineteenth-century British utilitarian Henry Sidgwick, had said before: "Such affection as is produced by deliberate effort of will is but a poor substitute for that which springs spontaneously, and most refined persons reject such a boon: while, again, to conceal the change of feeling seems insincere and hypocritical."[14] But in the context of the last forty years, the implications of this were much greater.

Popular arguments incorporated the theories of experts, but went even further. They claimed that if we could use our power of free choice to control the future, it would be foolish to try to do so. Love is too easily stifled by the very idea of being obligated (through commitment or otherwise). Indeed, the binding of love may be what destroys it—destroys the spontaneity that makes us want to keep loving and doing the deeds of love.

It was often said, therefore, that to commit ourselves to anything but the most temporary and superficial actions or relationships is to fail to take account of how much we do change in a lifetime. It is to fail to understand the nature of human emotion and human learning. It is also to court disillusionment, for it overestimates the objects of commitment, refusing to see that perhaps nothing is sufficiently worthwhile, and no one is sufficiently lovable, to withstand the gradual demystification which time brings. When the scales drop from our eyes, or the rose-colored glasses are torn away, we will know that we should not have invested so much of ourselves in this love or this enterprise. Even God may change our call through the grace of these realizations, releasing us from past obligations, opening our future to something new.

Still, these philosophical (and sometimes religious) arguments, although they may be corroborated by experience, can seem not fully and finally persuasive. Commitment remains a problem for most persons in the twentieth-first century—if not any longer "in principle," then "in practice." We do still anguish, for example, over how to keep commitments, once made, alive; how to prevent the slow ebbing of passion within them, or the gradual flattening of emotional bonds into sheer obligation or duty. Whatever the intensity of our love and our commitment, we do still encounter times of emptiness and distance in our pledged relationships. However full our lives have been made by choices of our roots and loyalties to our futures, we still find ourselves hungering for more—more "at home-ness" in our world, more "interest" in our lives, more fruitfulness in our engaged activities. The question of this century is whether or not our theories can be deepened, our understandings expanded, so that neither dead-end pessimism nor naive optimism will prevent us from growing into our loves and our unified lives.

In the late twentieth and early twenty-first centuries, philosophers have worked on theories that are in a sense "removed" from direct analysis of commitment and fidelity, but they do not deny altogether the problems that continue to plague both the concept and the practice of these. Their basic theories appear also to assume something of what we generally mean by commitment. That is, these theories are not so much about freely undertaken promises, commitments, pledges, but about what "matters" in human life and love. Hence, for example, Harry Frankfurt explores what he finds is most meaningful in life, and focuses on what we "care about." This may or may not involve a *chosen* commitment, but it surely involves commitments that are "givens," in our bones because of family ties, longstanding political loyalties, or recognition of what it is we truly love.[15] Other philosophers like Charles Taylor also do not focus on commitment as such, but honor the importance of integrating our loves and our lives, of unifying our "selves" in a way that seems to require something that looks very like "commitment."[16] Agnes Heller proposes a view of the "map" of the individual self, one that depends on ratifying our most valued desires and loves, even with some form of self-determination, free choice, and again, what seems like commitment "by any other name."[17]

In the end, our efforts to understand commitment, promise-making, self-possession, and love of another may constitute a daunting challenge. It is not, however, rhetorically superfluous to focus on such concepts and even to search for their meaning in our experience. We may also find some guidelines for commitment that may serve self-understanding, honesty, and fidelity. For, as Frankfurt acknowledges:

> Even after we have recognized what it is that we love . . . establishing the defining necessities of our volitional nature, problems of course remain. We can fail what we love through ignorance or ineptitude; and we can betray what we love, and thereby betray ourselves as well, through a shallow indulgence that leads us to neglect its interests and hence to neglect our own.[18]

THE CONTEXT OF FAITH

The questions, then, that remain central to our understanding and practice of commitment are both empirical and theoretical. They rise out of our experience, diverse as it is, shared as it is. Ultimately, the questions connect—or at least can connect—with our deepest religious and theological concerns. This is because some of our commitments are so deeply interwoven in the fabric of our lives that they inevitably touch our most fundamental convictions and our most fundamental loves. And some commitments not only intersect with these beliefs and loves; they are expressions of them.

There is much I will not do in this book. There are many aspects of commitment that I will not explore, many problems I cannot here address. I will do little, for example, with the sociological issues or with the issues usually treated by psychologists. But theological issues present a special case. Explicitly theological, and even religious, language appears for the most part only at the end of this book, in the final chapter. This smacks of a *deus ex machina* introduction of considerations of faith. But at least I must say in the beginning that I do not intend it to be such.

Rather, there is a sense (though not an uncontroversial one) in which the entire book is intended to be theological. I am exploring the questions of commitment, and of love and freedom and human time and obligation, within a context of faith. What I say will, I hope, have significance for those who do not share such a context. For those who do, I am not writing of a God who hovers only at the margins of our experience, granting special solutions to the most difficult of our questions. Nor am I pointing to a faith that invigorates or comforts us apart from, or in spite of, our real struggles, our failing loves, and our loves unto death.

Our experiences in relation to commitment constitute in large part our vantage point for understanding God's commitment to us and God's desire for commitment from us. If God breaks into our lives in a way that shatters the limits of what would otherwise be our experience, this change or expansion of limits becomes part of the experience we must try to understand. Moreover, if by God's gift, God's grace, our experience of commitment is changed, transformed, it is still our experience that must be pondered and in relation to which we must make our choices. The considerations I attempt regarding the "way of fidelity" (and equally so, the way of discerning when commitments no longer bind) can be considerations of the *way in which grace works* when it works in our lives of commitment.

To think that such a focus turns us in upon ourselves, preoccupied with our own "experience," unable or unwilling to open to God's own self or even to one another as sharers in the human community, is to miss the inner potential of our experience. Neither God nor human persons are reducible to our experience of them; but in our experience may lie the promise of transcendence of ourselves, of access to communion and friendship with what is other than ourselves. Moreover, just as special revelations (whether through sacred scriptures, or through the voice of the community, or through other sources) may illuminate all of our commitments and enable us to covenant forever, so our philosophical reflection on our experience of commitment can, as Paul Ricoeur testifies, "set off the horizon of significance where [God's word] may be heard."[19]

I assume from the beginning, therefore, a theological framework, specifically a framework drawn from Jewish and Christian traditions. Call it "faith seeking understanding," or call it "thinking about" questions that are so important they press themselves on our minds and hearts. I do not debate doctrines of the human person or of grace or sin or eschatology, though from time to time they may appear. But, then, I also do not delineate (let alone justify) the complete ethical theory that is necessary for adequate philosophical support of some of the positions I take. What I do here is partial, and because it requires a whole, it assumes one. I think its requirements are not such, however, that what is here in part will be useless to those whose view as a whole differs in some ways from mine.

I proceed, then, because for women and for men old questions regarding commitment remain, and new ones continue to emerge. These are fundamental human questions, although they are etched in the material of our particular lives, formed by the prejudices and opportunities of our times. Because such questions are ours as much as they were those of Antigone or Lear, of Solomon or Job, of Mahatma Gandhi or Martin Luther King, Jr., of Joan of Arc or Dorothy Day, it cannot be superfluous to look at them anew. Sometimes it is better simply to live the larger questions we face, rather than talk about them or even think about them too much. But sometimes we cannot live them as questions at all (cannot bear them or cannot allow them to be opened for us) unless we reflect upon them. This book risks the latter alternative regarding our experience of commitment.

There are, of course, no final answers to most of the questions I will trace and no complete solutions to the life-situations I will describe. It is possible, however, to do two things whenever we come face to face with unanswerable questions for which we need answers (without which we cannot go on) and irresolvable situations which we must resolve (or we cannot endure). It is possible, first, to expand our horizons—to push back the dimensions of the problem, gain light by turning it this way and that, broadening its context into a larger world and life. It is possible, second, to enter more deeply into the questions—to take a lantern, as it were, and walk into what may ultimately be a mystery to us, but which we do not deserve to call a mystery until we have walked into it as far as we can go.

CONCRETE EXPERIENCES

There is one more step for me to take in this introductory chapter. In order to explore the problems and possibilities of commitment, I need to give some concrete, specific examples—whether fictional or real. I will begin, then, not with a definition of commitment (although I will eventually come to that), but with examples of the kinds of experiences I am attempting to understand. I will try to name and to reflect upon, for instance, the story of Stephen and Ann.[20] They have been married for twenty years and now are deciding whether they must separate from each other. It is not clear what words can be said between them, words that can carry the whole reality of long years of marriage marked overall by peace and fulfillment, though ongoing struggle, and then sudden illness, and developing distance between them, mutually inflicted pain, and growing repugnance and despair.

I want to consider, too, the story of Stephanie, a successful graduate student who stands at something of a crossroads in her life, searching for clarity about her future. She has multiple realistic opportunities for positions in her field, yet she dreads the day to day tedium of working in a laboratory. She is attracted to work abroad where life may be austere and difficult, but it will, she thinks, never be boring. She is also torn between crossing to new continents and remaining in the same city with a fellow student for whom she has feelings of budding love.

And then there are Barbara and Tim—fifty years of love, of toleration, of battling and irritation, of mellowing, of shared pride each in the other, of combined shoulders' bearing long nights and long years of children's sickness and confusion and wandering, and finally children's shattered dreams as well as achieved fulfillment. They will continue their life together, but have paused to reflect on its meaning and its future.

Harriet is struggling to balance her work in a social service agency with the care of her children at home and her decision to return to school with her desire to spend more time with her husband. Is "commitment" some kind of label that becomes a bludgeon in describing her anguish at trying to hold all the pieces of her life together, trying to be responsible yet humanly free?

Is commitment the term that helps us to understand what is missing when Robert cannot see Maureen's desperate need for him to stay this last time that he has returned home to her and their baby? Can lack of commitment describe the deep chasm in him that makes him choke with fear at the loss of one more subsistence-level job, and impels him to run again? And what is it, then, that goes out of Maureen's heart when the baby dies, and Robert is gone, and she decides to die, too? In the face of such tragedy, can a word like "commitment" be for Maureen more than empty, more than insulting, arrogant, unseeing?

Is there an understanding of commitment that illuminates the life of Karen, seeking as she does to belong to God, to share life in community with others, to quiet the restlessness of her heart and the urgent anxiety of her compassion? Can exploring commitment help her understand what it is for which she yearns, what she dreams of, as her life stretches out before her, and her love grows for God and God's people?

Can "commitment" ever tell the history of Jill's and Sharon's love, discovered so gently, nurtured so carefully, tested so stormily, promised so hopefully? What about the fragile trust between Jack and Beth—trust that the lives they pledge will succeed in blending together, that their marriage will not end in the same courts as the marriages of so many of their friends? Does "commitment" have enough power to name the loyalty that Jane has vowed in her heart to her African American sisters, knowing what it will mean for her to carve away at her own white racism?

And there are the stories of Carey's decision to leave a religious community after twenty-five years, as well as Sandy's halting efforts to be a serious artist, Kevin's lifelong agony in dealing with an unrequited love, Rachel's gradual acceptance of institutional rigidity and oppression, and Cheryl's conflict of loyalties between government administration and the people whom the government is meant to serve. If there are any connections between ordinary lives and those of a Dorothy Day or a Martin Luther King, Jr., between our own labors and those of a Madame Curie, what are they? What are the connections, as well, between the mistakes and failures in our relationships and those of everyone else, great and small?

Can our thin understanding of "commitment" reach all the way to the power and the tenderness, the everydayness and the awesome mystery, of what we recognize as the covenant that God makes with human persons? Does that covenant have anything in common with our relationships with one another? Can it help us understand the stories of special bearers of the promise of God—like Sarah, who laughed, Hagar who wept and cried out, Miriam who conspired to save her brother Moses and thereby saved the people, like Mary, who stored up her fear and accepted it, and made the fulfillment of the promise possible?

The point, of course, is that all of these relationships, varied and particular as they are, do have something profoundly similar at stake. It is this common element that gives rise to common questions. This book aims to be about real lives, real persons, real human possibilities and limitations—but about something at the heart of these lives that can be named, lest we miss it. The name is less important than the reality named, but a name helps us to attend to the reality.

But why should there be a whole book about aspects of our experience that, despite the seeming poverty of our language, we do nonetheless call "commitment"? Only because herein lies a tale of great proportions. The examples I have given are not simply reported facts about people's lives. They hint at some of the most relentless questions with which people live—the anguished or merely nagging uncertainties that people carry into crucial decisions, the surging hopes and expectations as well as the sad longings for what might have been. Examples like these suggest that what we call "commitments" seldom are, at least in our time, settled facts of our identities—not until they are lived to the end, or left behind for something better. Commitment may indeed point to some of the most profound and problematic, uncharted but graced, aspects and areas of our lives.

Chapter 2

The Meaning of Commitment

Commitment is a problem for us because by it we attempt to influence the future, and by it we bind ourselves to someone or something. Two quite different customs in contemporary society illustrate dramatically how this is done. If I am arrested by the police and wish to avoid jail while I wait for my trial, I may be able to post bail and so be free until my date in court. In giving money as bail, I am declaring my intention to return for my trial at a future time, and I am binding myself to return on penalty of forfeiting my bail money. In a wholly different setting, when two persons marry in our society, it is the practice of many to exchange rings. "With this ring, I thee wed . . ." symbolizes the expressed intention of each to love and to share the life of the other into the future. It symbolizes, moreover, a bonding whereby each gives to the other a claim to the fulfillment of that intention. These examples hold a key to the meaning of commitment. If we look at them closely, we can come to understand what we are doing when we make a commitment.

I find myself hesitant, however, to narrow our focus so quickly to these examples. We need a wider perspective from which to view them. There is, I suspect, something important to be gained from letting our minds roam a bit, trying to see the broadest possible sweep of the forms commitment can take in our lives. This will have the advantage of preventing premature closure on just one meaning for commitment. It will also help to keep any one dilemma of commitment from overwhelming us, or any one celebration of commitment from seducing us into complacency.

15

Indeed, the history of the human race, as well as the story of any one life, might be told in terms of commitments. The history of civilizations tends to be written in terms of human discoveries and inventions, wars, artistic creations, laws, forms of government, customs, the cultivation of land, and the conquering of seas. At the heart of this history, however, lies a sometimes hidden narrative of promises, pledges, oaths, compacts, committed beliefs, and projected visions. At the heart of any individual's story, too, lies the tale of her or his commitments: wise or foolish, sustained or broken, fragmented or integrated into one whole.

SURVEYING THE HORIZON

Think again, then, of all the ways in which we experience what we with some seriousness call "commitment." Sometimes these are not immediately evident in one person's life at any given time. When Sheila, for example, thinks of commitment, she tends to focus only on the one area of commitment which right now is difficult for her. Every day she lives with the more and more pressing question of whether or not she should persuade Joshua that they must divorce. Every day she agonizes over her responsibilities through marriage to her husband and to their children, to God, and to herself. But she has many more commitments than these, some that intersect with them, some that compete with them, and some that are not in question in relation to them at all. For instance, Sheila is committed to certain truths and certain principles. From the day she had her first insight into what she now describes as the "equality" of women and men, her conviction has grown regarding this truth. She can no longer act as if she did not believe it. She cannot turn back and live out the roles in her life as if she had never seen the reality of herself and all women in a new way.

Sheila also believes deeply in the obligation of persons not to harm one another unjustly. Her perception of the value and need of persons in relation to one another goes beyond this, to a desire and a sense of responsibility positively to help others. She has often said, "Life is hard enough for anyone to get through. I figure we can't do it alone. We have to help one another." Her compassion is based on conviction, and it does violence to her not to take account of others' needs—especially Joshua's, her children's, and the people she meets in her volunteer work and the political action groups to which she belongs. Genuine caring and compassion serve to motivate her involvement in organizations that oppose racism and violence and that promote economic rights and peace.

There is also a sense in which Sheila is committed to herself, though she is almost afraid to think in these terms. Her growing anger at what she perceives to be Joshua's indifference to her and to the children keeps generating in her mind the question of whether this is how she is meant to live. The frightening realization of how destructive her marriage has been to her keeps pushing her imagination to find alternatives, "ways out."

The story of Sheila's life and commitments could go on and on. But even a brief glimpse into it enables us to begin to see the many different forms and complex interconnections possible in our commitments. There are, of course, commitments to other persons—some made explicitly, some assumed implicitly. But there are other kinds of commitments, too. For example, there are what can be called "intellectual" commitments: to specific truths and sometimes to "truth" in general (a commitment that can undergird a pursuit of truth wherever it is to be found). There are commitments to values: the value of an institution, or the life of a family, or so-called "abstract" values like justice, beauty, and peace. There are commitments to plans of action, whether specific projects or life plans such as "living in accordance with the Gospel," or programs of vengeance, peaceful revolutions, or "being a good mother."

The appearance of commitment in our lives is even more extensive and nuanced than this, however, and more elusive when we try to encompass it within our overall perspective. There is, for example, a kind of unrecognized commitment, one that serves as an important background for almost everything we do. We are not explicitly aware of it (or of them, for there may be many such commitments). We may never bring it to a level of consciousness where we can reflect on it. This kind of commitment serves to *constitute* part of the very horizon against which we interpret everything. It may be a commitment that psychologists could describe as "basic trust," or one that philosophers could name a "presupposition." It may be one that any of us might recognize if and when it is brought into focus: for example, taking for granted that the law is to be respected, or valuing without question the progress of human education, or assuming that things should "make sense" whether we understand them or not. These kinds of commitments, prior to any explicit recognition of them in our conscious awareness, can be called "pre-reflective" commitments.

But if "commitment" can appear in all of these forms, what is the common meaning that keeps it from being empty as a term? Some clues emerge from what we have just seen. In our ordinary language, commitment seems to include a notion of *willingness to do something* for or about whatever it is we are committed to (or at least to protect it or affirm it when it is threatened). Suppose I ask, for example, what truths I am committed to. I soon discover that there are many truths that I hold, affirm, am convinced of, but am not "committed" to. What can this mean? I may say of some insight of mine or some conviction regarding a state of affairs or a direction to be taken that "I would not stake my life on it." This could mean that I am not completely certain about it, or it could mean that, though I am certain, it is just not important enough to me to *do* anything about it. It is not important enough to me to let go of anything else for the sake of it (let alone lay down my life for it); it is not important to me even to use my energy trying to defend it through argument.

A willingness to do something seems, moreover, to follow upon our sense of *being bound* to whoever or whatever is the object of our commitment. Our very selves (to greater or lesser degree) are tied up with this object, so that we do not just appreciate it or desire it, but we are in some way "identified" with it. Our own *integrity* seems to demand that, under certain circumstances, we do something. The object of our commitment has a kind of claim on us, not one that is forced upon us but one that is somehow addressed to our *freedom*. Even when we do not feel very free regarding our commitments, when we feel bound "in spite of ourselves" or against our other desires, there is still a sense in which our own initiative is involved when we act because of that commitment.

In continuing to survey the many forms of commitment and to probe the elements common to them all, we need to ask further about the relation of free choice to commitment and the importance of pre-reflective commitments for the commitments we are aware of making. Now, however, may be the time when it is more useful to take seriously my lantern metaphor and enter the deeper regions of one form of commitment. To do that, it helps to identify a kind of "prime case," a central form of commitment—one from which all other forms derive some meaning. *Commitment to persons,* when it is *explicit and expressed,* offers just such a "prime case." And it will bring us back to our two examples: the posting of bail and the exchange of wedding rings.

"PROMISES TO KEEP . . ."

By explicit, expressed, interpersonal commitment I mean promises, contracts, covenants, vows, and more. These commitments provide a prime case for understanding all of the forms of commitment, because the elements of commitment appear more clearly in them. We recognize an obligation to act in a certain way within these commitments more frequently than in any others. Moreover, it is in these commitments that we most often confront dilemmas and the inescapability of wrenching decisions, and where questions of love, of time and change, of competing obligations, seem more acute. The very explicitness of promises, or covenants and contracts, places the experience of commitment in bold relief and offers the best chance for understanding it.

There are interpersonal commitments, of course, that are not expressed in any explicit way (at least not in the beginning). For example, some roles that we fill, or relationships in which we participate, entail commitments, but they become ours without an original choice on our part. We are born into roles such as daughter or son, sister or brother. Some friendships grow spontaneously and seem to need no promises. Other roles we assume by explicit choice and usually through some external expression—familial roles such as husband or wife, sometimes mother or father, and professional roles like physician or teacher. Even roles we do not at first choose, however, can be understood in great part through understanding the roles we explicitly choose, for roles of whatever kind usually at some point require a free and explicit "ratification" or "acceptance."

The Making of Promises

The first thing we must do in exploring explicit, expressed commitments is to ask: "What takes place when we commit ourselves in this way?" What did Sheila *do* when she married Joshua? What will actually *happen* in the moment when Karen vows to live a celibate and simple life within a community dedicated to God? What does Ruth *effect* when she signs a business contract? What *takes place* when Dan speaks the Hippocratic Oath as he begins his career as a doctor? What *happens* when heads of state sign an international agreement regarding the law of the seas? What *happens* when Jill and Sharon pledge love and friendship for their whole lives long? What do Barbara and Tim *do* when they place their names on the lease renting their new apartment for a year? What do any of us do whenever we make a commitment to another, whenever we promise, whenever we enter or ratify a covenant?

We can ask this question of our previous examples of posting bail and exchanging wedding rings. What is happening in each of these cases? In both, I am "giving my word" to do something in the future. But what can it mean to "give my word"? It is surely not like other things I could do regarding future actions. It is not, for example, like a *prediction*. If it were, I would not be *responsible* for the future turning out as I said it would, except perhaps in some limited situations like that of a weather forecaster, who is not responsible in the sense of being able to control the weather, but who might be considered irresponsible if she did not show professional competence in forecasting. "Giving my word" is also not like making *a resolution,* where I may indeed feel responsible to do what I resolved, but where my obligation would be only to myself (to be consistent in carrying out my decisions), not to another to whom I had given my word.

When I post bail, I give my word that I will return for trial. I declare to someone that I will do this in the future, and I bind myself to do so by giving my money as a guarantee of my word. When two persons exchange rings in a marriage ceremony, they declare to each other their intention to act and to be in a certain way in the future, and they give a ring as a sign that their word has been given and that they are thereby obligated to it.

To give my word is to "place" a part of myself, or something that belongs to me, into another person's "keeping." It is to give the other person a claim over me, that I will perform the action to which I have committed myself.[1] When I "give my word," I do not simply give it away. It is given not as a gift (or paid like a fine), but as a pledge. It still belongs to me, but is now held by the one to whom I have yielded it. It claims my faithfulness, my constancy, not just because I have spoken it to myself, but because it now calls to me from the other person who has received it. My money is still my money when I give it as bail. That is why it binds me to come to trial, lest I lose what is still mine. A wedding ring is not just "given away." It belongs somehow to both partners, for it signifies a word that is "the real" in the speaker, begotten, spoken, first in the heart. Belonging to the speaker, the word now calls from the one who has heard it and who holds it. "What is mine becomes thine," but it is also still mine. It is still my own self, though I have entrusted it to another. That is why I am bound by it, bound to it, and bound to the other.

When I make a commitment, then, I enter a new form of relationship. The root meaning of "commitment" lies in the Latin *mittere*—"to send": I "send" my word into another. Ordinary dictionary uses for "commitment" include "to place" somewhere (as "to commit to the earth," or "to commit to prison," or "to commit to memory"); and "to give in charge," "to entrust," "to consign to a person's care" (as in "to commit all thy cares to God"). When I make a commitment to another person, I dwell in the other by means of my word.

Much of the time "all" that we give is our word—not money, not rings, not special tokens that "stand for" us. We stand in our word. Still, when we give just our word, we search for ways to "incarnate," to "concretize," to make tangible the word itself. It is as if we need to see the reality of what is happening. A good example is when we sign our name. Our word within a contract is sealed by placing ourselves—in the form of our name, written by our own hand—on the document. In one ancient Syrian form of blood covenanting, a man was required to write his name in blood on material which was then encased in leather and worn on the arm of his covenant partner.[2] Other rites of blood covenanting went even further, attempting to mingle the blood of one with another. Blood was the sign of life, and it was one's own life that was entrusted to the other in a sacred self-binding ritual.

When words seem too weak to carry the whole meaning of a commitment, sometimes we turn the words into chants, as if by repetition they become more solid, more visible in transfer. There is an ancient betrothal ceremony among the Berber tribes where the couple alternates in a song that continues for hours:

> I have asked you, I have asked you, I have asked from God and from you.
> I have given you, I have given you, I have given you if you accept my condition.
> I have accepted, I have accepted, I have accepted and agreed . . .[3]

Commitment, then, entails a new relation in the *present*—a relation of binding and being-bound, giving and being-claimed. But commitment also points to the *future*. The whole reason for the present relation as "obligating" is to try to influence the future, to try to commit ourselves to do the actions we intend and promise. Since we cannot completely do away with our freedom in the future (think of the gambler who must choose again and again to keep his promise or not), we seek by commitment to bind our freedom, though not destroy it. How can commitment do this?

By yielding a claim to someone over my future free actions, I give to that person the power to limit my future freedom. The limitation consists in the fact that I stand to lose what I have given in pledge if I fail to be faithful to my promise. I stand to lose the property I have mortgaged, or the bail money I have posted, or my freedom to travel if I am imprisoned for breach of legal agreement. I stand to lose my reputation, or the trust of others, or my own self-respect, if I am unfaithful to even an ordinary and fairly insignificant promise. I stand to lose another's love, or my home, or strong family support, or my sense of honesty and integrity, or my sense of continuity within a culture and religion, if I betray or finally break a profound commitment that is central to my life. I stand to risk the happiness of someone I love, if my fidelity is needed in a commitment made for the sake of another. Sometimes we know fully what we stand to lose, what binds us to our commitments; sometimes we learn what it is or has become only when our fidelity is seriously in question. It is clear that commitments vary, so that in some commitments we stand to lose little; in others we stand to lose everything. Above all, however, as we take our own word seriously, we always stand to lose a part of ourselves if we unjustifiably betray that word.[4]

If we stop here, accepting this as the full meaning of commitment, we are vulnerable to all the dangers regarding commitment that we saw in the first chapter. On the one hand, we can see the glorious possibilities of commitment—of gathering up our future in a great love, of belonging to another in a self-expansive way; and we may move too hastily into commitment for commitment's sake. In so doing, our one great commitment can end in a grand but empty and finally destructive gesture. On the other hand, the thought of yielding to another a claim over us—great or small—may intimidate us, make us afraid that any commitment we make will narrow our possibilities, leave us with no "way out," give us claustrophobia in a life walled in by obligations and duties.

The essential elements of interpersonal commitment *are* an intention regarding future action and the undertaking of an obligation to another regarding that intended action. But in order to see a reasonable place for it in our lives, and to be able to discern *how* and *when* commitment obligates us in specific circumstances, we need to think about the purposes that commitment can reasonably serve and the limitations that it must necessarily have.

A Remedy and a Wager

The primary purpose of explicit, expressed interpersonal commitments is to provide some reliability of expectation regarding the actions of free persons whose wills are shakable. It is to allow us some grounds for counting on one another. As Hannah Arendt observed, "The remedy for unpredictability, for the chaotic uncertainty of the future, is contained in the faculty to make and keep promises."[5]

Commitment as it appears in the human community implies a state of affairs in which there is doubt about our future actions. It implies the possibility of failure to perform acts in the future that are intended, however intensely and firmly, in the present. "Without being bound to the fulfillment of promises, we would never be able to keep our identities; we would be condemned to wander helplessly and without direction in the darkness of each man's *[sic]* lonely heart, caught in its contradictions. . . ."[6] Ours is not the instinctually specified and determined course of animals insofar as they have no freedom; ours is not the unshakable course of the freedom of God.

Because our wills are indeed shakable, we need a way to *assure others* that we will be consistent. Because we know our own inconsistencies, we need a way to *strengthen ourselves* for fulfilling our present intentions in an otherwise uncertain future. Yielding to someone else a claim over our future actions provides a barrier against our fickle changes of heart, our losses of vision, our weaknesses and our duplicity. By commitment we give ourselves bonds (and give others a power) which will help us to do what we truly want to do, but might otherwise not be able to do, in the future. A remedy for inconsistency and uncertainty, commitment is our wager on the truth of our present insight and the hope of our present love.

Insofar as promise-making provides assurance to others and strength to ourselves, it facilitates important aspects of human living. It is a device upon which personal relationships depend (in one form or another) and which political life (short of tyranny and total domination by force) requires. It undergirds the very possibility of human communication, for it is the implicit guarantor of truth-telling. As Erik Erikson insisted, "A spoken word is a pact. There is an irrevocably committing aspect to an utterance remembered by others. . . ."[7] It is interpersonal commitment (in a social contract of one kind or another) that has been the instrument of structures designed negatively for *mutual protection*—each person from the other, or a group from an outside threat; or designed positively for *mutual gain*—economic or cultural, through shared labor or property, shared knowledge or aesthetic enjoyment. I need not say again that it is commitment that serves to initiate (sometimes) and sustain (sometimes) *companionship and love*. It is commitment, too, that resides at the center of much of the history of religion, whether in the form of primitive bargains with feared and hidden gods or of a personally offered covenant: God giving God's word, assuring a people of a divine unshakable will, calling a people to their own consistency in freedom and love.

Limitations on Binding

If we are ever to sort out how and when we are obligated by our commitments, we must have some way of determining their limits. Unless Sheila, for example, decides that there is no way, ever, under any circumstances, that she can justify divorcing Joshua, she needs to be clear about the *extent* of her obligation to him and to their marriage. If all of our commitments are absolutely binding, then we shall expect to be overwhelmed by their competing claims, with no way to resolve them or, ironically, to live them faithfully in peace.

Obviously, not every commitment that we make is of equal importance to us or equally comprehensive in its claim on us. We do set limits to the obligations we undertake. Almost all of our commitments, for example, are provisional in some sense; almost all are partial, conditional, relative. It must be so. In fact, we might well ask whether more than one commitment (at least at one time) can ever be, without contradiction, absolute.

Sometimes there are limits within our commitments of which we are not aware. That is, it is possible for us to think mistakenly that we are committed wholly to something or someone when, in fact, we are not; or the depth of our commitment may be much less than we thought it to be. We are in these instances, like the apostle Peter, surprised at our easy betrayal of what we presumed was our one unquestionable commitment. On the other hand, sometimes we are surprised in the opposite way when we discover, like Judas, that we are more committed, more bound, to someone than we realized; what we assumed was relatively superficial or marginal to our lives shows itself to be profound and unforgettable. In either case, we may weep bitterly at our discovery and be filled with remorse or with gratitude for what it reveals.

There is perhaps no remedy except time and experience for deficiencies in our own self-knowledge. It is, however, possible to be more reflective about the limits we *intend* (legitimately and necessarily) to include in our commitments. To understand limits is not always to diminish a commitment but might, rather, serve to focus it, to allow it to share in the overall power and hope of a committed life.

It is too soon to try to work out all of the ways in which our commitment-obligations relate to one another. But we can see some general relationships in this regard, and at the same time gain an understanding of the possible limits of commitments. The terms that are useful for this are terms like "conditional" and "unconditional," "partial" and "total," and "relative" and "absolute." These pairs are not mutually exclusive, so they tend to blur into one another at times. Nonetheless, they help to articulate how much we yield in claim to another.

If a commitment is *conditional,* it obligates only under certain conditions. Sometimes we make commitments where we very clearly stipulate the conditions under which they will be binding. I promise to do something *only if,* for example, you reciprocate in kind; or *only when* the building code is met; or *only until* another worker can be transferred to this position; or *only if* my insurance policy will cover my expenses. An *unconditional* commitment, of course, is one in which I commit myself to another "no matter what" conditions prevail. Thus, for example, I may commit myself to "go where you go and stay where you stay," allowing no conditions to justify changing my mind or my sense of being obligated. We may discover that while it is the nature of every commitment to refuse to count some conditions as justifying a change in the commitment, most commitments are at least subject to sheer conditions of *possibility* of fulfillment.

A commitment is either "partial" or "total" depending on what is yielded for claim. It may be *partial* because of a limitation in time: until next week, or until the weather changes, or when I reach retirement age. It may be partial because it simply is "part" of something larger—as a vow of poverty may constitute part of a total commitment to service of one's neighbor. It may be partial because it yields a claim only to my property and not to my person.

We think of commitment as *total* when it somehow involves the whole person of the one who makes it. These are the commitments that constitute fundamental life-options. These may be some of the commitments we make to love other persons. When we try to describe commitments in this way, however, we soon meet difficulties in expressing our complex experiences. For example, how shall we describe the commitment to love another person that arises from the whole of our being, that is affirmed totally with our very lives, and yet does not entail a total availability to the other for the deeds of love? We hesitate to call such a commitment a partial commitment, and the hesitation has its own rich truth.

The notions of "relative" and "absolute" can be extremely helpful for understanding the nature and limits of our commitments. But these terms, too, hold a variety of possibilities that are not always easy to keep clear. Thus, *a relative* commitment is just that—*related to* another commitment. It is, at least to some extent, dependent for its meaning on the other commitment. It may be derivative from, instrumental to, or a participation in the other commitment. But even these terms, describing modes of relation between commitments, conceal complex possibilities.

There is a vast difference, for example, between purely instrumental commitments (commitments that are solely a means to some other end, some larger commitment) and commitments to love someone who is perceived as an end in herself, though an end (not a means) whose deepest reality is in relation to God. For example, Joshua may be committed to his wife and children purely because they are necessary to him if he is to sustain a certain status with his business associates. Or he may be committed to them because he sees himself as a dependable, responsible husband and father, and he knows that they need his financial and personal support. Or he may be committed to them because he loves them in themselves; but since he believes them to "live and move and have their being" in relation to God, his commitment to them is an intrinsic part of his commitment to God.

The easiest way to think of an *absolute* commitment is to equate it with an "unconditional" commitment. In this sense, however, some relative commitments could be called absolute (if what they are related to is the object of an unconditional commitment, and if the relationship is intrinsic and necessary). We might also equate absolute commitments with "total" commitments; but here we encounter the same sort of uncertainty that we met with the partial/total distinction. To keep the category pure, we might reserve it for commitments that are both unconditional and total. This would be the kind of commitment Gabriel Marcel describes as "entered upon by the whole of myself, or at least by something real in myself which could not be repudiated without repudiating the whole—and which would be addressed to the whole of Being and would be made in the presence of that whole."[8] However Marcel's way of putting it may strike us, it is not difficult to catch the central point of what he is describing.

I could, of course, simply stipulate meanings for these terms. That would be helpful for my use of them hereafter. However, since my real concern is to show the many ways in which we must and do set limits to our commitments, I prefer to leave the terms open to various correlations and to continuing refinement that accords with the many possibilities in our experience.

Distinctions such as I have suggested thus far may seem already overly refined when all we want to do is to live out our commitments faithfully or discern when they no longer bind. Fidelity and betrayal are not simple matters, however, and our lives always prove more complicated than we wish. Not every giving of our word to another is an unlimited yielding of an unlimited claim. Nor is every commitment as limited as our vague promises to "drop in sometime" to visit old friends. Through distinctions we may be surprised by some simple clearings in the forests of complication.

Chapter 3

Commitment and Love

Explicit, expressed commitments to love someone are not just prime cases for understanding what it means to make a commitment. They are also particularly clear cases for understanding what free choice can do when it comes to influencing within ourselves a human emotion like love. Presumably, the point of making a commitment to love is to do what all commitments aim to do: set up a relationship in which we are obligated to a word given as a pledge—obligated to keep on loving as we have promised into the future. Here, then, are all the questions we have previously seen of whether or not a choice now for the future can be effective in any way; and whether, insofar as such a choice is effective, it contradicts and undermines the love it intends to preserve.

Experience teaches us many things about commitment and love—things that, over the years, surprise us. We learn that we can love another person in a way that makes us want to commit ourselves and our love forever. We find that it is possible to love more than one person like that in a lifetime. We remember being unfaithful to our commitments to love, but also being more faithful than we ever dreamed we could be. We know that we considered breaking some commitments altogether, and sometimes did, and other times probably would have if circumstances had been different. We learn that fidelity is possible, though total innocence is probably not; that mutuality is possible, though complete sharing is probably not. We leave some commitments behind—for good reasons or bad, with freedom of choice or because it seemed there could be no "turning back."

Most of us who have lived long enough to accrue "tested" experience do not remain romantic idealists about committed love, but nor do we despair of it. In fact, we accept it as part of life, as etched in our memories and mingled with the marrow of our bones. It does not matter if memory is scarred with sadness or warmed and healed with joy (and for most of us, there is some of both). The history of committed love is still there, and it is not finished. Still within us, too, is the future of our committed love—within our imaginations as possibility, within our minds and hearts as life and as ongoing task.

It does not seem overly dramatic to say of our experience of commitment and love what Annie Dillard said of life in general:

> I am a frayed and nibbled survivor in a fallen world, and I am getting along. . . . I am not washed and beautiful, in control of a shining world in which everything fits, but instead am wandering awed about on a splintered wreck I've come to care for, whose gnawed trees breathe a delicate air, whose bloodied and scarred creatures are my dearest companions, and whose beauty beats and shines not *in* its imperfections but overwhelmingly in spite of them, under the wind-rent clouds, upstream and down.[1]

And if we are honest, we also say of our still-committed loves what Robin Morgan said: "'How come your marriage has succeeded,' they ask—as if, to paraphrase Sophocles, one could ever call a relationship happy until one knew its ending."[2] But the biblical Song of Songs plays in the background of our hopes: Love can be "strong as death"; there can be committed love "no flood can quench, no torrents drown" (8:6–7).

The kind of love and commitment I want to consider here is primarily the kind we find in romantic love or in friendship. I mean this in a strong and wide sense, rather than a weak and narrow one. That is, I mean any love that involves our whole affective self in some way—that engages us deeply, often passionately. I am not referring, however, only to "young love," romantic in the sense that a primary ingredient is sexual attraction or orientation toward marriage. The kind of love I am talking about can include these experiences, but it also includes the kind of rich and intense love that someone may have for close friends, or for groups engaged in a common cause, or for persons whose special needs awaken not only compassion but an urgent love, or for a community of persons, or, indeed, for God.

However strong and intense this kind of love may be, it is a love that experience teaches us can be most fragile. It is usually not grounded in a prior relationship such as kinship or professional responsibility (though it may be so, as the love of a parent for a child often shows). Hence, it usually provides us with the "hardest case" for commitment. This kind of love has always had a reputation for being fleeting. That is why it was considered necessary, if some such relationships were to continue, to stabilize them by moving them into institutional frameworks like the traditional institution of marriage or a vowed and regulated life in community. Today, however, in our society, not even this strategy offers the strong supportive base that seems needed. Institutions no longer "carry themselves." It tends to be the case, rather, that each loving relationship and each specific commitment must "carry the institution." Can commitment as such, however, really promise a future to love?

William Butler Yeats wrote knowingly of the anxiety of the lover:

> Earth in beauty dressed
> Awaits returning spring.
> All true love must die,
> Alter at the best
> Into some lesser thing.
> *Prove that I lie.*
>
> Such body lovers have,
> Such exacting breath,
> That they touch or sigh.
> Every touch they give,
> Love is nearer death.
> *Prove that I lie.*[3]

Lovers change, and love changes. What, if anything, can commitment do to enable them to endure? Is a "long and happy life together" something that simply either "happens" or "does not happen"? When Jack and Beth marry, is it a matter of fate or freedom whether they are faithful to the end? When Karen pledges friendship to a community of persons, is it out of her hands now whether she remains in this community "for life"? Should marriage, in fact, be construed as a commitment "for as long as we shall love each other"? Should friendship or community be formed only provisionally "until another love takes its place"? Can, or ought, freedom to give a law to love?

It is commonplace today to answer the questions I have just raised by some sort of appeal to the need to "work at" marriage or community. The assumption is, therefore, that we *do* have some power to make choices that will sustain our committed loves. With all of our supposed new wisdom in this regard, however, evidence mounts that either not many of us are making the right choices or love is too elusive for our decisions to bind.

It may not be superfluous, then, to reflect on our experience of making free choices and our experience of love.

THE EXPERIENCE OF FREE CHOICE

It is probably a mistake to assume that we are all frequently aware of exercising freedom of choice. On the other hand, some of us think we do make many choices in an ordinary day, and some of us can even remember making "radical" choices: ones that set the course of our whole lives in a profound way. In 1982, Carol Gilligan's studies of moral development in women showed reluctance among women to recognize their power to make choices and a corresponding tendency to interpret their lives as "drifting" into commitments, following the expectations and the decisions of others. One woman reported, for example, "As a woman, I feel I never understood that I was a person, that I could make decisions and I had a right to make decisions. . . . I still let things happen to me rather than make them happen, than make choices, although I know all about choices. I know the procedures and the steps and all."[4] Today, of course, many women would report more awareness of their choices, more intentionality in their commitments.

Whatever our history of decisionmaking, we can usually locate some experience of choosing, either at a level of trivialities or among basic, life-altering options. Even if we doubt our real capacity for freedom of choice, we generally live as if we had some power of decisionmaking. As Samuel Johnson once said regarding human freedom: "All theory is against it, all experience for it."[5]

Choice Is of Action

If we think, then, for a moment about any experience of making a choice, what do we find it to be?[6] First of all, it involves some selection among alternatives. These alternatives are always something that I can *do* (or at least think I can). They are always some *actions* of my own. For example, I have a choice between the alternatives of going to a movie or watching TV; of taking job A or job B; of marrying or not marrying, or marrying this person or that; of fighting a decision of the department of social services or trying to borrow money from a friend.

The fact that what we choose (or even consider choosing) is an action of our own is extremely important, even though it is not always obvious to us. We tend to think of ourselves as choosing between external "objects"—coffee or tea, job A or job B, this person or that. And it is true that in a serious sense these are what we choose. But, more accurately, it does not mean anything to say I choose these things or persons unless I mean that I am choosing some action of my own in relation to them. Nothing is effected, nothing happens, choice is an empty term, unless it means that I choose to *drink* coffee or tea (or to buy it), to *work in* job A or job B (or apply for it), to *love* this person or that one (or select her or him for my project, or call him or her on the phone). This is why free choice is called "self-determining," and the power of making free choices is called the power of "self-determination."

Choice Is of Desire (For an Action)

Deeper even than this in our experience of choosing is the fact that we never choose (or even consider choosing) any action of our own that we do not *desire* to do. Of course, this cannot mean that we only choose what we "feel like" doing or what we desire to do, in the sense that we want it "most of all" because it will give us the most pleasure. Clearly we have experiences of choosing some actions because they seem more responsible or because we feel others want us to do them (even if we would, from the standpoint of our other desires, prefer to do something else). It would be a mistake to interpret such experiences as if they are simply choices of duty versus desire, or choices of what we *do not want* to do versus what we *do want* to do. All of these options (if they really are options) are *desired by* us— for different reasons and in different ways, but nonetheless desired. We may desire to do our duty because we experience a profound sense of moral obligation, or because we fear reprisals if we do not do our duty, or because we like to be praised for being dutiful. Still, we do desire these options, and if we did not, we could not choose them. It simply is not possible to choose an action for which we have no desire whatsoever, no emotional "inclination." What begins to emerge from this view of our free choices is that what we choose, when we choose, is not only an external action of some kind, but always also an internal "action" of our mind and heart. We choose from among our very *desires* to act and our very *reasons* for acting.

This, of course, does not mean that we choose desires and reasons for acting in the sense that we "make them up" out of nothing. Quite the opposite. Desires and reasons are already present within us; we already see the reasons and are already leaning into the desires before we choose. Choice, when it is free, is the choice of one desire and reason (or set of reasons) over alternative desires and reasons. All of the alternatives exist in some sense within us prior to our choice. If I do not have more than one possible action, and hence more than one desire for action *already alive within me,* I have no choice to make. Choice is, therefore, my *ratification* of one desire (rather than its alternative), my allowing *this* desire (rather than its opposing alternatives) to issue in action. I choose the reason for the desire, too, for if the reason *necessitated,* absolutely determined, my ratification of one desire for action over another, there would no longer be a free choice at all.

I, so to speak, "identify" with one desire and the action which is its object, and I "let go of" the others (not usually in the sense of "turning off" the other desires, for they often continue; but in the sense of deferring their satisfaction—for now or forever). The difficulty we have with making choices is, in fact, often not with affirming one desire and action but with letting the others go.

What, then, does free choice *effect?* It effects action. It represents my power to take hold of my very understandings and desires and to identify with them *by my freedom* and to translate them into action. If it is sometimes the case that one desire is so strong that it "compels" me to act, then I do not make a free choice. I am, in this case, moved automatically by a power within me, but not a power whereby I determine myself from the center of my personality, my freedom.

Most choices that we make, of course, are more complex than this description shows. For example, the actions that we desire and choose are not necessarily external actions. They can be internal ones, as when we desire (to choose) to believe, or to remember, or even to desire (however strange that sounds, we *do* sometimes desire to desire). Moreover, we often have many reasons and many desires for each alternative we are considering in any given choice. The process of decision making, when it is done reflectively, is a process of weighing all of these, sorting them out, trying to understand and to evaluate them. When Sheila, for example, decides to file for divorce or to try some new way to improve her marriage with Joshua or to put off doing anything at all, she finds herself considering her desires for security, for ongoing love, for a home for her children, for freedom from bitter quarreling, for integrity in living her religious beliefs, for growth and personal happiness. These are desires which may in turn underlie fear and anger and hatred and hope and despair. It is not, I think, necessary here to sort out all the threads of the possible objects of her choice, all the movements of her mind and heart in relation to a lived situation, in order to understand the potential power of her freedom and the depths of her own self that are at stake in this decision.

Choice Is of Love (Ground of Desire)

But we still need to bring all of this analysis of free choice to bear on the question of whether or not we can or should make choices and commitments precisely to love. If we ask, first, whether *love* is something we choose, we find an important clue by pursuing the analysis of choice just one step further. There is, after all, one more "piece" that is needed if we are to understand the experience of free choice as such. It is suggested by asking: If in making a free choice we always choose an action of our own, for which we have some desire, where does the desire come from? We might answer this in terms of our personal history. Perhaps it comes from my learning as a child the importance of duty, or from my long years in this relationship which have made me cherish it or fear it. This is important information for coming to self-understanding in decision making. But it does not in itself provide the "missing piece" we need. That piece comes into view only when we realize that every desire is rising, here and now, out of an emotion that is more fundamental than desire. The fundamental emotion which gives rise to desire is love.

My desires for job A and for job B may be rooted in a whole series of other desires, but they are ultimately rooted in a fundamental love—a love of someone or something for its own sake. For example, I may desire job A because it pays well and is therefore a path to some of the things in life that I have always wanted for myself or for my family. My love for myself or for my family is therefore at the heart of what I choose if I choose job A. Or I may desire job B because I like the work and the colleagues I will have and the goals of the corporation. I desire all of this, again, because it is a way of loving myself; or of loving God, whom I see as ultimately served through this type and context of work; or of loving other people, to whom I can relate through this work in a meaningful way.

Without arguing this at great length, I want at least to suggest that every free choice ultimately includes a choice of what and how to love. Finally, every choice is a choice not only of my action, not only of my desire and my reasons for desire, but of my love and the reasons for my love. In order to test the plausibility of this claim, we need to look more closely at our experience not only of choosing but of loving.

THE EXPERIENCE OF LOVE

What is love? Not just "romantic" love, but what is any love? It is not uncommon for us to discourage the definition of love on the grounds that it has too many meanings for too many people. Nevertheless, we simply cannot hope to discern the possibilities of commitment to love without some shared understanding of love itself. We do not need to settle all of the questions that psychologists and philosophers debate regarding love, but we do need to consider some key issues for it in relation to commitment, and we do need at least a "working" description of the central elements in our fundamental experience of love.

Love and Feeling

A major issue for us is the distinction of love as an emotion from "feelings." It is true that people use both the terms "emotion" and "feeling" in a variety of ways, sometimes equating them, sometimes sharply differentiating them. I think, however, that I can identify meanings that will distinguish emotion from feeling and at the same time clarify the meaning of love when it is a matter for choice and commitment.

Most of us know quite readily what is meant if someone expresses the fear that her lover's feelings will change. There is a way of "feeling" when we love (especially when we begin to love, when we "fall in love") that experience teaches us will surely change, perhaps even disappear altogether. No amount of choosing, it seems, will make it otherwise. If this is what love is, we can hardly hope to commit ourselves to its endurance.

Most of us, however, do not equate love with feelings. In fact, it is almost a truism for us that love is "deeper" than feelings, that it is not a matter of "feeling" but of "willing," not a matter of feeling but of caring and of doing the deeds of love. We are, of course, brought up short if someone asks us, "But why do you care? Why do you do the deeds of love?" We answer, "Because we love," but we are then hard put to say more about what that means. We are also not without our doubts about the rhetoric whereby we so easily dissociate love and feeling.

Philosophers have tried to articulate our lessons about love and its transcendence of feelings. Robert Solomon, for example, argues persuasively that love is an emotion, and emotions are essentially distinguishable (though not always separable) from feelings. Feelings are occurrences that happen to (or "in") us. They come and go; they are like (and they include) physiological sensations and disturbances. Emotions involve feelings, but not necessarily so. We can have emotions without feeling anything. "One can be angry without feeling angry: one can be angry for three days or five years and not feel anything identifiable as a feeling of anger continuously through that prolonged period."[7] So, too, one can love for a lifetime—sometimes with feelings in accord, sometimes in discord, with the love, and sometimes with no feelings at all. "Feeling is the ornamentation of emotion, not its essence."[8]

We might not want to go so far as Solomon and call feeling only an ornament in relation to emotion. At least in the kind of love that is of primary concern in this book, feeling seems extremely important. It might be better to talk about it in terms used by Jules Toner: Feeling may be "integral" to a concrete experience of love, but not necessary or essential to it.[9] The love *can* exist when the feeling disappears, but not without our regretting its loss. Love is not feeling, and our commitment to love cannot reasonably be a commitment to feeling. Yet, as I think will become clear, we cannot ignore the relevance of feeling to love if we are to understand our possibilities of loyalty.

For now, however, what is significant is that love, as an emotion, is not a wholly passive occurrence within us. Like knowing (and unlike feeling), loving is something we *do*. But what is it that we do when we love? We may do deeds of love, but they are not the love itself (presumably, they flow from the love). What are we doing when we are simply loving?

Affective Affirmation

When I love you, I want you to be. I am affirming your very existence, your life, your well-being. I want you to be firm and full in being. I say yes to you according to my understanding of your truest reality. My affirmation of you is "affective." My own self affirms you in a way that goes beyond any mere intellectual or verbal affirmation. A sign that loving you is different from and more self-involving than just knowing you is that I am willing to do the deeds of love, insofar as they are called for and possible. (If they are not called for, or not possible, then a lack of deeds does not negate my love.) If I behold you to be in need or in danger, I move to help you if I can. If I love you with what Toner calls a "radical" love—that is, a love for you yourself, a love that is the root of my care for you, my joy in you, my desires for your well-being—I affirm you as I affirm myself.[10]

Affective Union

When I love you, I am in a special sense also in union with you. My loving affirmation unites me with you. Sometimes we miss seeing this aspect of love because we think of love as *a desire for* union. And it is true that love often gives rise to an intense longing to be with the one we love—to be closer in time and space, to share more fully and know more intimately. But we do not long for such intimacy with, nor are we "lonely" for, anyone we do not already love. The love itself is a union, which is not belied by its causing in us a desire for fuller union.

Affective Response

As affirming and as unifying, love is active. It is something I do. It would seem, then, to be something I can easily choose. Like every other action, I can select a given love by my power of free choice. But there is another aspect to my loving which makes it, in its beginning, not a matter of "simply choosing." That is, my love for you is "first of all" a response—a response to your lovableness, your value and beauty. This is the passive dimension of love. I must "receive" your revelation of yourself as lovable. Your self, or some aspect of it, must touch my mind and heart, awaken it, so that I respond in love. Not that you necessarily decide to reveal yourself to me, or even that you are aware that I behold you. It is enough for you to exist, and for me to encounter you.

Ah, but many will say: Love cannot be essentially a response to what is lovable—for it is the height of human love (and the ideal of Christian love) to "love the unlovable." It is only a selfish love that has to "receive" something, even a revelation of beauty, in order to love. There is truth in this objection, actually, but only a partial truth. To "love the unlovable" makes sense only if it means that we are able to or ought to love persons whose beauty is not immediately evident to us, whose lovableness is hidden by some terrible evil or some superficial distortion that occasions our inability to see. In such instances, we are not enjoined to love what is literally unable-to-be loved, but to believe what we cannot readily see—to believe that there is worth and beauty, dignity and lovableness, in a person as a person and as this unique person who claims our love. It can be enough for us to receive the lovableness of the other through the eyes of faith, human or divine. Such faith, of course, would move us to a love the deeds of which would surely include trying to see what at first we are unable to see. Hatred of another person, as Graham Greene suggests, may be "just a failure of imagination."[11]

My loving affirmation of you is, then, *a responding* as well as *a uniting affirmation*. It begins not with sheer force of "willing" to love, but in an "indeliberate, unfree response,"[12] a spontaneous reply to the reception of your lovableness. Love, therefore, is simultaneously passion and action, receiving and giving; there are two sides to the one coin, the one reality, of loving. What, then, is the power of freedom to influence love?

FREEDOM AND LOVE

Ray and Sarah have been together for five years. Their love has "settled" in that time into something less lyrical but more peaceful and sure. Is it their choices that have brought this to pass? Stephen and Ann, after twenty years of marriage and four children, say their love is "dead." The only emotions they share are anger and resentment; otherwise there is nothing any more between them. Could they have altered this course of their love by making different free choices? Susan has spent ten years living and working with a group that provides shelter for homeless poor. During those years she several times wept in rage and despair, and she almost left the group and the work for something less demanding and more likely to bring lasting results. Is this a story where freedom of choice has sustained compassion and zeal? Helen has fallen painfully in love with a man who teaches in the same school as she, and with whom she shares a love of literature and the arts in a way she has never been able to share with her husband. This new love is, she feels, a "great love, a classic love"—though it may destroy her marriage and both of their careers. Does she have any real freedom in relation to her old love or her new? Only Ray and Sarah, and Stephen and Ann, and Susan, and Helen know the answers to these questions; and even they may not be completely sure. What we can try to know, however, is whether *it is possible* that choices, made by at least some persons in some situations, can make a difference to love.

In its first awakening, love is not a matter of free choice. It is a spontaneous response to what is perceived as lovable. That we have seen. Nonetheless, I can influence love even in its beginning by choosing to attend to certain realities or not, putting myself in a position to discover lovableness if it is there, choosing to believe in the value of persons. Insofar as love is like a judgment of value, I can, as Robert Solomon says, open myself "to argument, persuasion, evidence."[13]

Even more importantly, once a love exists, it can offer itself (so to speak) to freedom. That is, my love can give rise to a desire in me to accept and affirm itself, to affirm the one I love, by my free choice. I, at the center of myself where I am free, can identify with my love— with this love or that, this way of loving or that, this action to express love or that. I can take responsibility for my love—not just be carried away by it or victimized by it.

My choice of my love can also shape the love. I can choose to believe in my love, even when my feelings vacillate. I can choose to pay attention to the one I love, looking again and again for the revelation that nurtures my love. I can choose to try to modify my emotions and feelings whenever they conflict with my chosen love, or to ignore them, or to give them "free" play in my mind and heart. I can use my imagination, or perform activities, in a way that will help to "de-fuse" contradictory emotions which get in the way of my loving. I can choose to interpret the words and actions of my beloved, my own feelings, or our situation together, in a way that undermines my love or that helps to sustain it. I can choose to do the deeds of love, and order my life, in a way that is conducive to my love's continuance and growth.

Love is not, therefore, something that merely "occurs" in me, wholly beyond my power of freedom. I do experience being able to "work at" loving relationships, being able to gather my own spirit and nudge it this way and that, gaining wisdom and power for myself and my love. I make decisions about ways of expressing my love (for example, with regard to my sexuality) that will, in turn, affect the form of the love. And other choices that I make, not directly regarding my love, but for the sake of it—choices about my work or my many relationships—have also consequences for my love.

Yet I do not have anything like total power in respect to my love. I experience myself as fragmented and conflicted, conditioned as well as self-determining, "swept away" as well as "self-possessed." No, there is no such thing as despotic control over any of my emotions by my freedom of choice. Belief in such a possibility probably rests on a faulty model of the human self, a popularized brand of Stoicism which would make reason the conqueror of emotion, rationality the mark of freedom—or the opposite, a runaway romanticism which would collapse freedom into my spontaneous emotions. It surely is blind to my complex experience—where I know that I can choose my love, but not always. I can shape my love, but oh, so slowly. I can cultivate my love, but only through long and patient attention. I can discipline my love and liberate it; but sometimes it still slips through my heart or disrupts my ordered life.

Insofar as freedom can influence love, however, it can affect its future. It seems that we can, then, make commitments to love. We need to explore more directly what that means.

COMMITMENT AND LOVE

Like any other commitment, a commitment to love is not a prediction, not just a resolution. It is the yielding of a claim, the giving of my word, to the one I love. But promising what? It can only be promising that I will do all that is possible to keep alive my love and to act faithfully in accordance with it. Like any other commitment, its purpose is to assure the one I love of my ongoing love and to strengthen me in actually loving. Given the challenges we have seen to the wisdom, if not the possibility, of commitments to love, this purpose bears fuller examination.

Purposes of Commitments to Love

Why should I want commitment if love rises spontaneously, and if I can identify with it by my freedom at every moment? Why should I promise to love if there are risks to the love itself in making it a matter of obligation? Only something at the heart of our experience of loving can explain this.

There are some loves whose very power in us moves us to commitment. "Love's reasons" for commitment are at least threefold, and they go something like this. First, like all commitments, a commitment to love seeks to *safeguard us* against our own inconsistencies, what we perceive to be our possibilities of failure. If we are not naively confident that our love can never die, we sense the dangers of our forgetfulness, the contradictions of intervening desires, the brokenness and fragmentation in even our greatest loves. We sense, too, the powerful forces in our milieu—the social and economic pressures that militate against as well as support our love. We need and want a way to be held to the word of our deepest self, a way to prevent ourselves from destroying everything in the inevitable moments when we are less than this. To give to the one we love our word, to yield to her or him a claim over our love, offers a way.

Love seeks more than this, however. We know that freedom cannot once and for all determine its future affirmation of love. No free choice can settle all future free choices for the continuation of love. Yet sometimes we love in a way that makes us yearn to gather up our *whole future* and place it in affirmation of the one we love. Though we know it is impossible because our lives are stretched out in time, we long to seal our love now and forever. By commitment to unconditional love we attempt to make love irrevocable and to communicate it so. This is the one thing we can do: initiate in the present a new form of relationship that will endure in the form of fidelity or betrayal. We do this by giving a new law to our love. Søren Kierkegaard points to this when he says, "When we talk most solemnly we do not say of two friends: 'They love one another'; we say 'They pledged fidelity' or 'They pledged friendship to one another.'"[14] Commitment is love's way of being whole while it still grows into wholeness.

Finally, love sometimes desires commitment because love wants to express itself as clearly as it can. Commitment is destructive if it aims to provide the only remedy for distrust in a loving relationship. But it can be a ground for *trust* if its aim is honesty about intention, communication of how great are the stakes if intention fails. The decision to give my word about my future love can be part of converting my heart, part of going out of myself truly to meet the one I love (not part of hardening my heart because of excessive fear of sanctions if I break the law that I give to my love). My promise, then, not only verbally assures the one I love of my desire for constancy; it also helps to effect what it assures.

Law "Against" Love

It is, of course, true that this law can prove to be "over against" the love it binds. There are some commitments that are antithetical to love. Jean-Paul Sartre's description of the "pledge" that a group may take in order to resist its own dissolution comes to mind. Because each member of the group fears his or her own capacity for falling away, they choose to give the group power to "kill me if I secede."[15] What this kind of commitment does is establish in the group a "reign of absolute violence over its members." What holds the members to their pledge is a dread of "what the others will do to me." The only way for freedom to counter the forces that pull us away from one another, back into isolation, is to build structures of "Terror," our only guarantee of faithfulness to our word.

Sartre may have intended only a stark portrayal of what it means to entrust oneself to another by undertaking a commitment. Yet the language of violence and fear, of coercion and terror, seems to contradict the whole point of commitment to love. Whether or not initially motivated by love, commitments to individuals or organizations or institutions that claim loyalty primarily on the basis of fear cannot serve love. Indeed, there are frameworks that we enter "for love" and which prove to be structures of violence— whether physical or psychological. When this happens, however, the power we give to another by giving a claim over ourselves becomes a destructive power, an alienating power, not one that calls forth affective affirmation or that nurtures union. Loyalty oaths are then exacted to substitute for trust or to compensate for love's loss; they add bitterness to distrust, and they do not bring back the love.

Indeed, to commit my love is to give it a new law, to obligate it, to bind it and its desires. But if love is to commit itself wisely, it must be possible to give itself a law that corresponds to the love. The claim I yield must be a claim on me to do what I deeply want to do, what I most profoundly ask of myself. Then it is true, however, that this law can prove to be "over against" the love it binds. Love can, after all, cease to want its own law. The law of commitment may become, then, a burden to love, a structure of fear and violence, a destroyer of love.

But it may also be "over against" my love in the sense that every human love needs at times to be coerced, or at least persuaded, to be faithful. Love, in this instance, can still welcome its obligation. Law can serve the love. Duty, then, comes (as Kierkegaard's defender of marriage commitments maintained) "not as a stranger, a shameless intruder," but "as an old friend, an intimate, a confidant, whom the lovers mutually recognize in the deepest secret of their love."[16]

Laws in the Service of Love

If the law that commitment brings to my love is to do what it is intended to do (that is, help and not hinder the love), we may need some guidelines for our making of commitments to love. For example, however much it is true that every choice, and every commitment, involves uncertainty and risk, it is nonetheless not wise to entrust ourselves to another without some reasonable grounds for trusting that other. Though the flights of first love may carry us to a desire to give all—either to another person or to an institution or community of persons—the claim that we yield must be appropriate, fitting, to the relationship that is possible between us. The trustworthiness and, in an important sense, the worthiness of the recipient of our promise are matters of legitimate concern.[17] So also is our own capacity for keeping the word we give (for though we avoid calculations of success in this regard, we must have some grounds for hope that we can fulfill what we promise). There is much to be said for clarity about the conditions that should characterize most of our commitments. As Sir David Ross observed, even in the case of "private promises it would often be well to express the conditions more exactly than we usually do."[18]

The "law of commitment" as I have referred to it thus far is the obligation undertaken to do what we promise. If the promise is to love, then the law of commitment is the obligation to love. But we hardly ever commit ourselves just to love. For the sake of our love, we commit ourselves to a "framework" of love; we stipulate what will be expected as signs of our love, as deeds of love, as efforts to make love continue to grow. By assuming certain frameworks for love (such as friendship, or marriage, or membership in communities of various sorts), we commit ourselves to whatever we understand essentially to constitute those frameworks.

We generally require that human relationships be governed by certain norms or ethical principles—principles of justice. Frameworks for commitment, then, ought to be subject to norms of justice. In most of the commitments we are exploring here, this means that the frameworks, the "laws" of commitment, need to be in accord with principles like respect for persons, like equality and mutuality and equitable sharing. The issue of justice in making, as well as in keeping and breaking, commitments—in particular, commitments to love, and to the frameworks of love—is one to which we shall have to return.

Here we remain with many cautions and questions. How great the caution that is born of self-knowledge and acceptance of the limitations of a beloved. How pressing the questions of self-fulfillment and other-centered love; of happiness and duty; of the need for equality and the desire for mutuality in our commitments to love. Both naive idealism and tired skepticism threaten our commitments with indifference and distrust. But love will not be denied its desire for commitment, nor life its hope in it. And, as I shall continue to try to show, commitment *can* support the possibility of a free and faithful love.

Chapter 4

The Way
of Fidelity

It is all well and good to come to some understanding of the meaning of commitment and love, but we are still left with the question of *whether* every commitment must be kept; and, for those that must be kept, *how* we shall manage to do so. We do not need much experience to know that we cannot always simply "will" to be faithful and succeed. I am quite sure, too, that different words regarding fidelity are needed by different persons in different situations. What is freeing and strengthening for one may be debilitating and harmful for another. In this chapter, I am concerned about insights that may be necessary for us when we *want* to keep a commitment; when we discern that we ought to, and we want to, live it to the end. In examples I have used before, I am trying to find words that will speak to Henry's yearning to come alive once more out of the grim apathy that marks his relationships and his work; to Rachel's fear of the disillusionment that threatens her dedication to education and to ministry; to Sheila's faint longing to restore the life she once had with Joshua and the children; to a community's eager (or even grudging) desire to be faithful to their call and to their promises. I am not at all sure these same words can be spoken to Stephen and Ann, if their love has indeed died; or to Harriet, if some of her commitments have been made out of feelings of guilt and sustained without acknowledgment of the conditions of human limitation. In any case, what I want to explore might be called the "way of fidelity."

We generally share, I think, an unspoken conviction that there is a "way of fidelity" that is more than holding firm out of a sheer sense of duty. When we give our word in a commitment to love, we

49

undertake an ongoing obligation, it is true. But we presume that our love will, overall, exceed our need to be bound by duty. In fact, when we pledge our love and our friendship, we believe that the duty we undertake will not substitute for the love we give, but serve it.

Duty can hold us in relation when all else fails. When our hearts are dry and our vision is clouded, when our memory is confused and our hope is eclipsed, then duty—our sense of obligation in relation to the word we have given—holds us to the deeds of love and to attentiveness to new springs of old love within us. But the whole "way of fidelity" is not like this. Or if by some rare exception it is so for us, then we shall need equally rare heroic courage, extraordinary "grace" of character to traverse it.

No, the overarching role of duty in our commitments to love is more likely to be the indirect and paradoxical one whereby we are obligated to find ways to continue loving, but ways that are not themselves dependent only on the obligation we have undertaken. There is a wisdom for faithful loving, a wisdom to which duty calls us but which duty itself does not provide. I want in this chapter to bracket a consideration of the force of obligation or duty as such, and to look more generally to the possibilities of fidelity in our commitments to love. I will not try to offer "how to" formulas, though I assume that the more we can understand of the nature of fidelity, the richer will become the options in its regard.

EXPLORING THE WAY

One way to explore the meaning and potential of fidelity as a human achievement is to put it against the background of two elements of the human personality that have become centrally important for us today and yet seemingly problematic for the value of fidelity. These are the elements of freedom (which we have already examined to some extent) and of "process" (our experience of constant change, not only in the world around us but in ourselves). Freedom may be essential to making commitments, but what happens to it when we "have to" keep the commitments we have made? Commitment is our way of bringing freedom to bear on unpredictable changes in our feelings; it represents our attempt to make love endure, to prevent the kind of process which would dissipate love and obscure the self we want to be. But does freedom really have this kind of power? Once again, can a choice made here and now actually reach to our future actions? If so, to how much of our future can we commit? The whole of it? Ten years? A year? A day? An hour? A minute?

Insofar as commitment succeeds in affecting our future, does it remove the possibility of process in our lives and in our relationships, thus also preventing growth and creativity? What sense does it make to cut off some possibilities, setting limits by our commitments to one possibility rather than another? Is not a large part of our future always unknown, so that undreamt-of possibilities may yet open to us, and we may change in ways we cannot foresee? We can begin to answer questions like these by exploring our experience of "human time"—of our lives stretched out into the past, the present, and the future. This may seem an unlikely place to look, but at the heart of this experience lie clues to the possibility of our changing, yet being faithful—or even of our changing in order to be faithful.

In a way, an exploration of the relation of freedom and commitment to time and process is a continuation of our exploration of commitment in relation to freedom and love. Before, my question was whether love can be influenced by free choice (whether, for example, Stephen and Ann could have altered a love that became resentful and angry, or whether Susan's sustained compassion for the homeless is the result of her free choice). In pursuit of an answer, I tried to probe the nature of love as well as of freedom. Now, with the same kind of examples, my question is whether choice has any power in relation to time; and if it does, whether *within a* freely made commitment there remains any room for future freedom of choice. In other words, is there still the possibility of process and change, not in spite of commitment, but because of it? From an examination of the experience of love, I want to shift now to include an examination of the experience of time.

The Experience of "Human Time"

A kind of folklore exists among us that attempts to mark the time of our commitments—to predict the time of our troubles as well as of our jubilation. Perhaps it parallels popular psychology, coming in part from observation, in part from our desire to contain the otherwise unpredictable factors in our lives. We console ourselves, for example, with reminders that the "first year" of any committed relationship is always the hardest, or that "after ten years" of anything (including marriage) there is bound to be a crisis. Whatever the accuracy of application of these theories, they are our acknowledgment that time is intrinsic to our experience of commitment.

How could it be otherwise? Commitment is our way of trying to give a future to a present love. It depends upon the power of the past (promise) to influence the present (fulfillment). It aims to strengthen us, so that our love will endure through time; to assure us, so that we may trust within time; to integrate love, so that one day's fears do not threaten another day's desires, or one year's weakness overwhelm another year's strength. Yet it is not immediately obvious whether commitment is, therefore, a way of resisting time (of making love endure in spite of time, as if there were no time) or of embracing time (giving love a history by giving it a future).

Clearly commitment can be related to time in more than one way. The manner of its relationship probably depends to a great extent on how we think about it. If we think of time as a threat to love, then we see our commitments as preserving love against the ravages of time. If we think of time as an opportunity for love to grow, we aim our commitments to ensure for love the time it needs. If we look upon time as something to be spanned, we seek by our commitments to reach across it without being touched. If we consider time as truly integral to commitment itself, we try to learn time's mysteries and to prepare for its fruits.

Our selves and our relationships are so complex that it is inevitable our experiences of time will vary. They vary not just among different persons, but in the life of each of us. For example, we can experience one aspect of our life as moving "quickly," another moving "slowly," or both moving at the "same time." We grow rapidly weary of working at a task in which we make slow headway. Or our imagination rushes wildly ahead while we wait what seems years (but may only be hours) for an event to occur.

Even our images of "rapidity" or "slowness" signify different things in different situations. We call the time of our boredom "dragging," and the time of our contentment "slow, stopping for a moment." The time of our anxiety "flies by," but so, too, does the time of our happy excitement. It is possible to experience time as draining, emptying, shattering, and simultaneously filling, completing, integrating. All of this is true because we live on so many levels: knowing, feeling, imagining, remembering, loving. We live embodied and enspirited lives, filled with hopeful opportunities and fearsome obstacles, with everydayness and "fullnesses of time." The models that philosophers have offered to explain time probably all fit some dimension of our lives. We live in "cyclic" patterns; there are seasons to our love. We live with "linear" development, positive or negative; our malice or our integrity matures. And we know the "spiraling" aspects of our lives, where there is "nothing new under the sun" and yet all is new, nothing as it was before.

It may be obvious how all of these kinds of experiences of temporality, of lived-time, are critical to the potential meaning of commitment. Think of the menace of boredom's time, the seeming endlessness of a future that holds no joy. Think of the difficulties of blending the lives of two persons whose temporal rhythms are radically different. Think of the changes that make us aware of time and the new tasks that emerge for incorporating changes into a partnership or community. Think of the potentially massive practical consequences of patterns of patience or impatience within a committed relationship.

Presence and the "Between"

Acknowledgment that temporal process is involved in commitment does not in itself yield much insight for fidelity, however. We need to look more closely at the fabric of our experience of time. It is not given in one moment or even a series of moments, passing, as ancient writers thought, "from the now to the then." For living beings, time cannot be reduced to the measured time of clocks and calendars. Nor is it the same as space, one moment outside another moment, like one inch outside of and next to another. "Lived time," as the philosopher Henri Bergson insisted, is *in* us, as the time of a tree is in its trunk (and can be measured by counting its rings) or the time of a rolling snowball is in the snow that it gathers as it goes. We can understand the story of our lives and our commitments in beginnings and endings but also, and in some sense more importantly, in the "between" of their processes. It is the "between" that is constitutive of what comes to be. Thus, "to the artist who creates a picture by drawing it from the depths of his soul, time is no longer an accessory; it is not an interval that may be lengthened or shortened without the content being altered. The duration of his work is part and parcel of the work."[1]

We catch a glimpse of the "between" of process by looking closely at what Maurice Merleau-Ponty called a "primary experience" of time, "right now," "today." In my day, today, morning may be past, but it is not just a memory. Evening is still to come, but it is not a remote future. The whole day is my "present," and it reveals human time as a "field of presence." Morning and evening, my immediate past and immediate future, are my two horizons. Though I cannot touch them, they are both still present to me. My experience is of the "future sliding into the present and on into the past," in a day that still

> weighs upon me with all its weight, [that is] still there, and though I may not recall any detail of it, I have the impending power to do so, I still "have it in hand." In the same way, I do not think of the evening to come and its consequences, and yet it "is there," like the back of a house of which I can see only the facade, or like the background beneath a figure.[2]

What is given in the experience of "my day" reveals something of the meaning of time in the whole range of my life. No moment, event, or desire ever becomes simply past—stored in the memory, perhaps to be recalled, or left as a silent trace in my body or my mind and heart. My past is in me, but not just as something I have acquired, not a mere accumulation, like the snow in the rolling snowball. Time in me is a continuity of interpenetrating elements. My life is not like a roll of cinematographic film that can be stopped at any point and understood in still pictures, isolated frames. The meaning of the past is modified with each new present, and the meaning of the present can finally be understood only in the future. The ultimate meaning of the promise I make today, for example, can be clear only at the end of my life; and the meaning of my life at its end will be different because I make this promise today. Today I cannot undo the mistake I made yesterday, but I can decide to forget it or to compensate for it, to transcend it or to mire myself in remorse. I cannot fully preserve any moment, sad or joyous, just as it is, unchanged by what follows; yet I *can* preserve it in some ways, allowing it to burden or lighten my present and to form and color my future. My future, too, changes my present and my past, not just when it comes, but while it is the future which I anticipate with eagerness or dread, with playfulness or bitterness or daring.

In a terribly important sense, time is for me an aspect of my very self—my self expanded into my past and my future. My present outruns itself, drawing my past in its wake and already impinging on my future. The experience of my time can be like listening to music, where the notes are connected to one another. There is no void between them; each note of the melody is understandable only in relation to the notes before and after, all held together by a beat, by echo and expectation.

Whenever my life is experienced as so fragmented, so disjointed, that my present seems to collapse in upon itself, flattened without a sense of past or future, it becomes painful, empty, shallow in its meaning. There are, of course, other kinds of moments, when time seems to have stopped, but these moments are full of the past and the future (whether happily or sadly). Not isolated moments, they appear, rather, to encompass the whole of time. They are like notes that hold the whole of the song.

The implications of all this for our understanding of fidelity are great. Before we look at them, however, we must focus more specifically on the process that is involved in living a commitment. Just as time is part and parcel of the work of the artist drawing his picture, so fidelity has to do not just with the making of a commitment and its final fulfillment, but with what comes "between." With commitment, a *new relationship* begins in the present. And it is this relationship, bound by my word, that *moves into the future.* How it is lived between its beginnings and its fulfillment (or betrayal) determines and constitutes its meaning and its final form—no less than the time of the artist is within his finished work.

Process and Freedom

The nature of the "between" of fidelity is unique to each commitment. How Susan lives out her commitment to the homeless is different from how Jack and Beth live out theirs to one another. It is even different from the way in which any of Susan's coworkers live out their commitment to the homeless poor, despite the fact that she and they share intimately in a common project. The process of living out any commitment is influenced by countless factors in our historical context, in our own selves, and in the complicated interaction between the partners of a commitment. Moreover, the use of our freedom in response to these factors is unique in its deepest intention and actual consequence. Still, there are some things that are true of all our commitments, some things we can say in general about the role of freedom in determining the nature of the "between."

First, many of our fears (though not all) of losing our freedom and cutting off our possibilities through commitment are unfounded. We simply do not, for example, have the power to *eliminate* future free choices even in regard to what we promise. Free choice can directly affect only present actions; it has only indirect control over future ones. I may decide (and even promise you) now, tonight, that I will rise tomorrow morning at 6:00. A sign that my choice tonight does not settle my action for tomorrow is that when the alarm rings at 6:00 a.m., I have another choice to make. I can choose tonight to plan to get up at a certain time tomorrow; I can arrange the circumstances so that I am likely to do so; I can intend to do so and obligate myself to do so; but ordinarily it is not possible for me to *necessitate* my rising at 6:00. So, too, when I commit myself today to a project for the year, or to lifelong friendship with you, I will have many new choices to make as the year, or our lives, unfold.

Commitments do limit the possibilities of our future in a serious way, of course. For example, as my committed relationship moves into the future, I must choose again and again to ratify it or not; but because of my commitment, the choice is not a "neutral" one. Insofar as the commitment remains binding, *my new choices are qualified* as choices of fidelity or betrayal.

In addition, some of my commitments do, in fact, *render certain otherwise viable options impossible* for me. Despite our experience today of long lives in which long-forgotten possibilities return again (new careers, new marriages, new causes, new educational opportunities, new ways of having children), we do pass some crossroads where there can be no turning back. We do, by our choice of commitments, close off some options. Even if they appear again in some form, they are not the same as they "might have been." Self-process for me is in some way restricted by my commitments.

In another way, however, that self-process is liberated. It is true that "decision" entails a "cutting off" of some alternatives. But such a cutting off is necessary if we are to actualize anything.[3] When we are faced with mutually exclusive alternatives (ones that simply cannot all be realized by us at once), we shall do nothing at all if we cannot commit ourselves to one and let the others go. The old adage is true: "It is impossible to run in all directions at once." Without commitment in relation to some possibilities in my life, I am left only with potentialities. Commitment limits self-process, but it is also what makes it possible.

Yet commitments are not only choices between competing possibilities. Their primary meaning is not the negative one of "letting go" but the positive one of realizing something new. This means more than allowing one possibility to be actualized rather than another. It means opening up a whole "line" of process in which more and new possibilities unfold. Some options emerge only as process goes forward. We do not choose by our commitments entire finished "programs" for relationship. The major commitments in our lives do not carry completed blueprints, fully charted maps; they are not well-constructed games or finely tuned machines for which all the options exist ahead of time. Commitments lead to genuinely new possibilities which are not foreseeable in the beginning. We cannot know them ahead of time, because they do not exist (even as "real" possibilities for choice) ahead of time. A large part of the "between" of commitments must, then, be what Henri Bergson calls "invention"—coming upon new points of decision, inventing new solutions to problems, fashioning new opportunities by entering more deeply into the very process that is chosen.

We are like the sculptor who envisions and chooses what she will make. We sketch a design and select the clay, the model, the tools. But in the sculpting, something new emerges, not wholly foreseen or heretofore understood. Our commitment to the work is not cancelled or postponed; it is lived out by deciding for it at each creative juncture. Fidelity to it can include letting it emerge under our hands, responding to our medium, modifying our sketch, choosing new tools, and learning more fully what was given only partially in the spark of our original vision.

But it is not only art that involves a process of vision and invention, or that actualizes one possibility which in turn opens to another and another. The same is true of our commitments to work, to friendship, to political life and more. The "between" of the time of a committed love does not rule out process but is constituted by it. Insofar as it is a "living" process, its future includes what is truly new.

"Presence" and the Way of Fidelity

I began these general considerations of our experience of time and the nature of human self-process in order to seek clues for understanding fidelity. At least two such clues emerge: the nature of human time as a "field of presence" and the ongoing need for freedom of choice in the process of living a commitment. Above all, these are clues for understanding why, as I claimed earlier, the "way of fidelity" cannot and need not consist only or even ordinarily in keeping commitments out of a sheer sense of duty.

By returning now to the distinction between the "way of fidelity" and the fulfillment of commitments strictly out of duty, I escalate its importance beyond even what I have said before. Of course, everything depends on what one means by "fidelity" and by "duty."

I have, I hope, already made clear (and will do so in more detail later) that, as I understand it, duty can play an extremely important role in holding us faithful to our words. This, after all, is part of the central point of commitment. Yet there are some commitments where "sheer duty" does not seem enough. Gabriel Marcel pointed to these when he distinguished "constancy" from "fidelity."[4]

For Marcel, the difference between constancy and fidelity is the factor of "presence." When I am "faithful," I perform the deeds of love in a way in which I am "present" in them. I continually struggle to overcome the feeling of "staleness," "absence," that threatens commitments through time. When I am only "constant," I perform the promised deeds of love with a kind of inert conformity to the letter of the law of my commitment. In some commitments it may not matter whether all I can muster is constancy. In others, however, we may consider ourselves actually "faithless" if we cannot sustain a kind of "presence" in our actions. We recognize this when a friend learns that we do the deeds of love only because we feel bound by an earlier pledge. She may be moved to say to us, "with an intonation that can have infinite variations: 'Don't think you are obligated to. . . .'"[5]

There need be no opposition between constancy and fidelity, however. Sometimes, indeed, all we *can* do is remain constant. But it is possible for constancy to be a part of fidelity, a way of struggling to be present until we are capable once again of a fuller experience of love. Constancy can, then, even represent the greatness of our love: our decision to stay in relation, to affirm the one we love, to do the deeds of love whether we "feel" present or not. In this case we *are* present in our actions, not just conforming to an ideal of ourselves, or avoiding a sense of guilt, or pretending we are not indifferent.

When, however, constancy becomes separated from fidelity, the relationship becomes a shell of what it was intended to be. Now conformity to duty is truly "inert," and we veer dangerously in the direction of resentment, rancor, hypocrisy, and despair. The past of our promise is split off from the present of its fulfillment, and we begin to have to mask the loss of aspects of ourselves that no longer exist. This is the prospect that Sheila fears if she stays within her marriage to Joshua without some change in the relationship.

The "presence" of which Marcel spoke referred to a kind of "being there," being present to those to whom I am committed. We can express this in personal *spatial* terms like being "with," being "near to," "before," "in the presence of" you whom I love, and being "here" in the activity I perform. We can also express it in terms of personal *time:* being present "now," *holding together the past and the future in a present process.* It is the importance of this temporal dimension that we are likely not to see, and it is what I want to stress in probing the meaning of fidelity. There are crucial ways, too, in which the spatial and the temporal depend upon one another. Perhaps we try to express their coming together in a term like "abide," as in "abide in my love," "abide in my promise." Our question is: How shall we do this? What is the "way of fidelity"?

GOING ALONG THE WAY

Like many other aspects of human life, fidelity can perhaps be understood best when we understand what threatens it. Because of this, I am turning to three kinds of experiences which constitute potential crises for fidelity to committed love: (1) Whatever the wholeness of our desire to be faithful, whatever the greatness of our love that gives rise to such a desire, whatever the lovableness of the one (or ones) to whom we are committed, we can still experience conflicting loves, conflicting new desires, strong pulls to abandon one commitment in order to take up another. (2) However sure we are of the beauty, the worthiness, the truth in our beloved, we can still enter a "dark night" of both vision and love that tends to put this lovableness in radical doubt. (3) Whatever the intensity of our experience of life and love and fullness of time within the process of commitment, we can still feel it sliding into emptiness, and distance, and the deadening poison of our own indifference. What are we to make of these seeming dilemmas for fidelity?

Conflicting Desires

Helen has fallen painfully in love with Abe. Yet she still loves her husband, with whom she has been reasonably happy and has shared the parenting of a child. Karen, after five years in a religious community, experiences a growing loneliness, even though she has found energy and love in her prayer and in community and in her work. She begins to yearn to renew her relationship with Carl, who still loves her and who would welcome her back to the engagement they broke six years ago.

We all know we can be pulled away from our commitments by competing desires. The intensity of old loves can return, and we begin to consider reversing our earlier decisions. Sometimes, moreover, it is possible to go back, to retrieve an alternative we thought we had left irrevocably behind. Then, too, a new love can always break upon our horizon. It simply is not the case that we can fall in love only once or that we can love only one person at a time. Sometimes our understanding of ourselves changes, and we become aware of needs we never knew we had, or we appreciate in a new way the importance of our own growth, of faithfulness to our newly perceived capabilities.

It is possible that some of our commitments ought to change in the face of new or renewed loves. I still want to defer a consideration of the discernment of obligation in this regard, however, and to continue to focus on situations in which we think we ought to, and want to, remain faithful to our present commitments.

Perhaps nothing substitutes in situations like these for having originally made the commitment with a "settled sense of decision." Though life is never absolutely "settled," we can make some decisions in which we do self-consciously "let go" what must be renounced if we are to embrace a certain love, and a certain way of living our love. It is possible, when we first undertake a major commitment, to reach a point in which we don't foresee everything that may arise in the future and handle it ahead of time, but in which we know enough to be willing to risk what we do not yet know; we accept the consequences of our decision, in both what it offers and what it rules out. Even so, we will still reach other moments when, like Karen, if we do wish to remain faithful, we must again (or at last) decide to "let go," to refuse to be distracted from what "is" by dreaming about "what might have been." In these moments, at least, there is no substitute for radical decision—renunciation and affirmation.

Yet decision in this sense is not just an appeal within me to my "will power." It is the recognition that there are certain ways I cannot allow myself to *think*. The key is more in my imagination than in my will. The same is true when I am faced not just with an "old" love but with a new one. Some form of decision is needed, the opposite of dreaming or drifting. The decision is not so much to force my will upon my actions or to wrench desires away from my heart, but to "stop" long enough to hear the voice within me that is most truly mine. If, halting there, I understand that I do not want to lose what I have pledged myself to and I do not want to betray what I have chosen to love, then I cannot (not even in my imagination) play games that will threaten that bond. I must not begin what will lead where I do not ultimately want to go. I cannot pretend that in this one aspect of my life (that is, in the relationship that conflicts with my commitment) there is only a present, and no future with which I must deal.

Of course, a hundred qualifications can be made to everything I have just said. Of course, it must not be taken to mean that every commitment to love must be isolated from all other loves, eliminating all other friendships and made to bear the whole meaning of my relational life. Of course, it cannot mean that refusing to "think" certain ways, to allow imagination to go in certain directions, entails my never reviewing present commitments and never imagining new futures. Of course, too, it offers only a glimpse of what serves at some points to go along the "way of fidelity" in the face of conflicting desires. It serves better if we add to it what follows.

The Loss of Original Vision

When we first "fall in love," the one we love is beautiful in our eyes. It does not matter that he (or she, or they, or it—in the case of a group, or a movement, or an institution) has quite ordinary features, even obvious deficiencies or impairments. These do not take away from (and may even add to) the beauty we see. "Romantic" love (with the same meaning that I gave it in the previous chapters) is love that rises from our whole self in response to an "original vision" of the beloved as beautiful, as wholly lovable. Such love may come all of a sudden—there *is* love at first sight, first meeting, first coming to know—or it may dawn slowly, as the one we love is gradually revealed to us in the beauty we perceive.

We are well aware, generally, that what we behold in this original vision is not all that we shall come to see in time. There is the danger both of underestimating and overestimating its importance. To avoid overestimation, we warn ourselves and others who are in love: "'Romantic vision' is not what is important, nor is the kind of love that depends on it." "Wait until you lose your rose-colored glasses." Some, however, like the theologian and writer Charles Williams, have worried more about the danger of underestimating the importance of the vision.[6] He feared that in our cynicism or caution we would fail to understand the significance of an original "revelation" and "vision," something on which the whole relationship might ultimately depend.

We tend, according to Williams, to make three fundamental errors regarding our original vision. They are errors of overestimation, but if we do not understand them, they will lead to errors of underestimation. We think that (1) the original vision will last, just as it is, forever; (2) that it brings with it an experience of love that is sufficient in itself; and (3) that the vision and the love are given only for the two of us (or however many directly receive it and share it).[7] Alas, all three assumptions are mistaken.

Regarding the first, the original vision does, indeed, not last. There is an inevitability to its fading. When it is gone, however, the question of fidelity arises, perhaps for the first time, and the question is: Shall I remain faithful to the vision I once saw but see no more? Shall I, in darkness, now *believe* in a light I no longer see? Everything depends on how we interpret the loss of vision. Usually we believe that we now see more clearly than we did before. "Now I see what he is *really* like." Now I see what this church, or this segment of the peace movement, or this profession, are "*really* like." In fact, we probably do know more about the ones we love than we did in the beginning—more facts, more limitations, more oddities; and we see that as persons they may be less profound than we thought, less motivated by singleness of purpose, less possessed of genuine charm.

There is also the possibility, however, that we actually see *less well* than we did originally; that what we have come to know is less centrally characteristic of this person or group than what we saw at first. One small habit of Ann's that irritates Stephen, for example, may loom larger in his perception of her now than anything else, so that the beauty that is still there is blocked from his sight. When sharpness of intellect or loveliness of face appear less brilliant or less striking, we may forget that these were only *conditions* for our original seeing, and what we saw was more than any of these alone. Or we may simply have grown "weary of wonders," as Chesterton said, or "tired of beholding beauty," in the words of Williams. "Beauty ceases, in one's own sight, to be beauty, and the revelation to be revelation."[8] Yet what we once saw was real, and remains real. The problem is with our seeing, not with the beauty of the beloved.

How shall we know which is the truth, which is the more authentic way of interpreting our now not-seeing? Do we see better now, or less well? After all, we *could* have made a serious mistake in first loving someone. But we can also make a serious mistake in now ceasing to love. There is no way of determining, with absolute certitude, the answer to these questions.[9] Both authentic and inauthentic original visions, both reality and illusion, fade. We need *some* grounds of credibility, some indication of the "reasonableness" of our belief or disbelief in the ongoing beauty of the one we love. Yet the *wager* of fidelity is in our choice to believe in the original vision now when we no longer see it. If we are right, the vision will be possible again in some form. If we are wrong, we may "prove to be, of all persons, the most foolish" (I Cor. 15:19).

If we once again begin to see, the revelation may be greater than it was even in the beginning, tempered though it is with reality in its mixture of beauty and ugliness, wholeness and limitation. And if the revelation is greater than at first, it may be followed, in turn, with an even greater not-seeing (a darker night or a too blinding, searing, bright day). It is not only mystics who learn the way of patterned glory and dark night and of new glory and new night. It is not only they who must discern the reason for the night or they who must activate new ways of seeing, more faithful ways of believing, opening larger capabilities of loving. It is not only they who can come to know how much we need the night as well as the day, and how great can be its glory and how moving its power.

Vision and disillusionment, learning and seeming unlearning also apply to our knowledge of ourselves. In the original vision we can think that we, too, are filled with glory in a way that will last; that we who before have been weak will now be strong; that we who before have been self-preoccupied are now completely freed; that we will be forever faithful, forever understanding, forever filled with love. This part of the vision fades as well. Yet it, too, may hold a truth and beauty to be believed in, a positive revelation about ourselves which we can dare to trust.

The second assumption we make regarding the original vision, thinking that our original experience of love in response to it is sufficient in itself, proves likewise to be inevitably false. Despite its importance for awakening love and for revealing something essential about the beloved and about ourselves, the event of the original vision and spontaneous love is not sufficient in itself. Even if it could last forever, it is not enough. The reason is that the vision (when it is authentic) is not so much about what exists now, but about what we can *become* together. It is meant to call us into a process of love and fidelity, not to let us settle into a present that is closed. The original "falling in love" needs ratification by our freedom along a carefully discerned way of fidelity. For it to come to be in all of its promise, we must learn a kind of "discipline of nonfulfillment," freedom's way of not destroying the future by mistaking it for something less or demanding it before its time.[10]

The third error, thinking that the original vision is "just for the two of us," is like the second in that it tempts us to close in on ourselves and on a fleeting bliss. Love, after all, is a gift, awakened in us first by the revelation of another (and when it is mutual, the revelation of one another). No gift, no "grace" of this magnitude, is ever given just for one, or just for two, or even just for our group. It is somehow given for all. The practical implications of this vary from situation to situation, from love to love. We learn, however, from our all too sobering experiences, that love tends to wither or be distorted when it is grasped too tightly, kept only for ourselves. Its growth in depth between us must be at once also growth into an open circle beyond us.

The original vision of our love and beloved comes early in a committed relationship. But its interpretation, and the choices we make in its wake, go far along the "way of fidelity." Choices in faith for remembered vision, in the present for the kind of present that has a future, in a relation that opens to wider and wider community, are choices that entail conversion of our hearts. In this lies part of the secret of truthful knowing and faithfulness in love.

The Loss of Presence

It may not be difficult to understand the problems we encounter in our commitments when competing desires arise or when we are disillusioned with the value and the beauty of what we love. However, there is another kind of problem for commitment that seems more elusive, less easy to define, and hence even more difficult to remedy. While all of the problems I have been considering are related to our experience of time, this third one depends most explicitly for its interpretation on our understanding of time.

Suppose there has been no real disillusionment in a commitment, no betrayal by the one we love, no loss of significance in the project we undertook. Yet lifelessness, apathy, or indifference gradually halt the momentum of our involvement. Something seems to die within us as well as between ourselves and what we are committed to love. We become more and more "absent" from the life of our commitment, disconnected from it as if we were only a spectator. We are like a driver of a horse-drawn cart who has experienced the horse becoming unhitched, running off and leaving us behind. We sit there, watching the horse go, admiring it for its beauty, but unmoved to catch it. We are no longer carried along with it in one shared movement; we are now only an observer.

Similarly, in our commitments it can happen that we seem to become "unhitched" from them, detached from the life in which we were engaged. The world goes on, our marriage or our work or our religious community or our political movement go on, while we in spite of ourselves seem able only to "sit there." Our committed life is in some way separated from us, and we become its observer. It is not that we judge it no longer to be worthwhile. We may even wish we could participate in it as we had before. But the process for us has stopped. It may still "work" for others—and we hope it does—but not for us. We may even continue to see clearly the beauty and the worth of the one we love, yet the "connection" between us is gone. We are no longer "engaged" in our love.

It is as if time, in relation to this commitment, has collapsed. Nothing is happening, nothing changes. The horizon has shrunk so that we begin to feel closed in. The past is cut off, and we stare at it as if from a distance. We see no future except ceaseless repetition. We sit or walk or even run as if in a vacuum. The most frantic of activities do not change the fact that we are observers of our committed lives, not participants. Sooner or later it is not just boring for us, or empty, or like a strange dream; it is oppressive and intolerable. We cannot live without a sense of process, cannot breathe without the expansiveness of a sense of time. The movement which characterizes *life* in time is gone.

Is there anything to be done in such circumstances that can "reconnect" us to our commitment? Of course we can decide that it is time to move on to something else—as, in some cases, it surely is. We can change our job, or take on different issues of social justice. We can accept the fact that some friendships must become more a part of our past than our present or future, even though we sustain them with sincerity insofar as we are able. We can acknowledge that we do outgrow some concerns and interests, even some relationships, or that they outgrow us. But if we want to renew the life of a commitment, to refuse to let it recede finally from the center of our lives, what can we do?

If we are to be "present" to our commitments, we must find a way to hold together their past and their future. We must find a way for free choice to prevent the loss of our love to the past and to sustain its engagements (even its spontaneous response) in the future we have promised.

Chapter 5

Conditions
for Presence

In the last chapter I said that I would not offer "how to" formulas for remaining faithful to our commitments. This does not mean that there are no practical conclusions to be drawn from what we have seen about the nature of fidelity. Understanding is itself "practical" when it helps us to interpret "why this is happening to me," especially in times of crisis. Knowing something about the elements of time and free choice within the fabric of fidelity also aids our recognition of practical conditions for fidelity, conditions that are conducive to our remaining "present" in our commitments. Let me reflect for a moment on what these conditions might be.

We need a way to keep us connected with, engaged in, our commitments. This is to say that we need a way to keep us present to the *object of* our commitments—what we love and have promised to love. But love, as I have understood it, arises from beholding, and thereby receiving, the lovableness, the beauty, of the one we love. As long as we see, loving is easy. When we cannot see directly, "face to face," we love by believing, by seeing "through a glass dimly." But this tells us that the way to keep love alive is not just to grit our teeth and say that we will love, no matter what. The way to keep love alive is to try to keep seeing, and our only hope of continuing to see is to keep looking. Even believing involves keeping watch, keeping vigil, seeing through memory and through hope. And when we do see directly, we can come to see better as we "attend" more carefully, more consistently—as we heighten our capacity to see.

Artists see lines and colors that the rest of us miss. Poets see depths in souls and patterns in life that the less poetic by themselves never glimpse. Saints see signs of God's presence in places most *of us* do not even look. And all of these—artists, poets, saints—*learn to see* better and better. So, too, lovers, who see what those who do not love cannot find, may learn to see better, learn to see more.

Seeing awakens love. Looking enables seeing. Fidelity entails decisions to look and to receive what is seen. Fidelity is, therefore, like love itself—both active and receptive—actively receptive, receptively active. It is not only a determined willing, nor sheer doing; it is also being done unto, being awakened, being upheld. It is not only presenting but receiving a presence. The conditions for presence, then, include what I want to call "refinements of receptivity."[1]

What might this mean practically? In the case of Susan, her relatively happy perseverance in her work with the poor and homeless is not just the result of her closing her eyes and willing with determination (though it is that, too, sometimes). It is the result of her seeing, again and again, the reality of persons, lovable and homeless and poor. She is like Meridian, the heroine of Alice Walker's novel of the same name, whose "dedication to her promise did not remain constant. Sometimes she lost it altogether . . . at other times [it] . . . came back strongly. She needed only to see a starving child or attempt to register a grown person who could neither read nor write."[2]

Or, in another example, it might mean that the only hope for Stephen and Ann's love is that they behold once again what it is in each other that holds the power to awaken their love. Their anger may be so great that they cannot "communicate" actively at all. They may have to begin by "contemplating" each other when they are in different rooms or safely behind a newspaper. Perhaps only in this way can they quiet the furor within them long enough to hear one another again, to be present sufficiently to negotiate either an end to their marriage or a renewal of their love.

The language of "contemplation," of looking and attending and trying to see, is no less relevant when we consider love for God. In fact, here we learn not to limit the forms of seeing and receiving—in regard to any beloved, but with a kind of quantum leap in regard to God. Whether the revelation of God we have received, or hope to receive, is immanent within us or transcendent beyond us, whether we expect it in the world around us or in our own desires and activities and imagination, and whether we look and listen by ourselves or in community, there is a need at least to "pay attention." This is not a matter only for mystics. Some of our hearts are kept alive by hearing again and again the stories of God's deeds; some by beholding "the dearest freshness deep down things";[3] some by pondering God's law; some by listening for "the blended note of the ten thousand things, the whine of wings," in the silence of God's brooding over the face of the waters of our world and our lives.[4]

Of course, there are ways of looking at another (at human persons or at God, at human communities or enterprises) that prevent love and that render us absent from our commitments. We may focus only on what we hate in another, what has always produced resentment in us. We may also look upon what we love with a "suspicious stare," the analytic and judging look which slowly drains for us the meaning from a project or the beauty from a person. We can be the spectator who sees only the absurdity of an external shell in what we view (like watching from a self-righteous distance a ritual that is sacred only to those who participate in it). These are "pinched" ways of seeing, ways of taking rather than receiving, projecting rather than beholding.

There is another way of seeing that can lead to mistaken judgment and love. One-sided, unreciprocated, watchful caring can be the mark of very great love, and through it love can grow. But it can also be the mark of a love that diminishes the self of the lover, that slowly takes from the eye its perspective and keeps from the heart its truth. In our struggle to allow the human persons we love to reveal themselves as they are, we walk between the Scylla of unfair judgment and the Charybdis of idolatry. We cannot be oblivious to limitation or to malice, yet we must, if we are to love, seek and seek again to see the lovableness which these should not hide.

There are, indeed, many obstacles to faithful seeing and loving. They are not only the obstacles of our self-preoccupation, our irrational fears and desires, our easy indifference, our cultural blindness. They are just as likely to be our limited powers of attention—our forgetfulness, our slips in focus, our weariness. But we are not, fortunately, totally helpless in these regards. Just as renunciation and resolution may help us with one set of obstacles, so there are ways around or through other obstacles. These ways will, I think, sound familiar.

MEMORY AND HOPE

I have talked a great deal about the relation between life and time. When we experience ourselves as most fully alive, then time, too, is "full." When life ebbs, our sense of time is of "empty" time, a burden rather than a moving support. When we are most deeply engaged in our committed love, it inhabits a "field of presence," the past reverberating and the future coming to meet us. How can we hold ourselves in this way—not in peak intensity, but nonetheless alive?

It is not as if we wake up one day and find that life has gone from a committed relationship (though we do sometimes seem to recognize its demise only after the fact). Death is a process just as growth is. In the telling words of Emily Dickinson,

> Crumbling is not an instant's Act
> A fundamental pause
> Dilapidation's processes
> Are organized Decays.
>
> 'Tis first a Cobweb on the Soul
> A cuticle of Dust
> A Borer in the Axis
> An Elemental Rust—
>
> Ruin is formal—Devil's work
> Consecutive and slow—
> Fail in an instant—no man did
> Slipping—is Crash's law.[5]

Forgetfulness is a way of slipping into death. Remembering is a way of growing into vision and love. Paradoxically, it is remembering that can give us a future. When, for example, the prophets of Israel called the people to remember their past—the promises made to them and their response—they thereby called them to remember "who you are." In this remembering, the people could be thrust toward a future: the future that had been promised.

Memories clarify and nourish our commitments. It is by memory that we are rooted in a living past—living because it is gathered into the present. Of course, not just any kind of remembering will do this. In fact, selective forgetting can sometimes be as freeing and faithful as it can at other times be faithless and self-deceptive. Moreover, we do change, and those whom we love change, and the situation in which we live changes—so that the kind of remembering I am talking about includes the possibility of seeing new meaning in the past as it unfolds in the present. "Anniversaries," for example, are not just moments to recall historical events and times. They hold an accumulated meaning, the meaning of what life within this committed relationship has become. They offer the possibilities of sorting out, letting go, or ratifying.

But if remembering is our way to hold the past in the richness of the present, hoping is our way of both embracing and expanding the horizons of the future. Grounded in the past and the present, hope is nonetheless our way of being free in relation to the future. Without a certain "flexibility" to our hopes, a refusal to "pin" them on set pictures or "fix" them completely to past images, the living movement of our commitment may end before its time.

If we are not to be "unhitched" from our commitments, the secret is to hold together our past and our future, but to do so in a way that does not leave us with something static and unchanging. Only if we are open to new meanings for the past can we risk flexibility in our expectations of the future. Without this kind of flexibility, we cannot sustain hope. For unless we are open to new meanings in the future, there can be no real future; there is only the past.

In this secret lies a twofold truth: Though the meanings of the past and future both change within a committed relationship, something endures. Along the "way of fidelity" we change, yet we endure; our relationship changes, yet endures. The difficulty we have in explaining this paradox is like the difficulty philosophers have in explaining the "enduring self." I am in every way different from what I was as a child, for example, yet I who was a child am now a woman.

The "I" who I am is neither an anonymous collection of "instants" with no continuing subject nor a "ghost in the machine," lurking behind all that I do and all that in me changes. No, it is *I* who *change;* it is *I* who am *changed.*

I am changed not only in spite of myself but by my own choices. Freedom *accomplishes* something in me, in time. It is I who love, who believe, who choose; and it is I who, though now loving, can choose to try to forget my love, to modify my love, to intensify my love. This does not mean I have total freedom. Some things seem to "happen" to my love without my choice (whether because of influences from outside of me or from drives, or lack of drives, within me). Yet insofar as I make choices about my love, including choices to remember and to hope in "us"—in our relationship, its past and its future—I change myself and the meaning of the relationship.

If, for example, I choose to forget my love, and so come to cease loving, my former love is not with me only as what I once did and once *was.* It is with me in the sense that I now *am* one who does not love because she is forgetful. And should I again decide to remember my love, to nurture it and to be faithful to it, my forgetfulness is not then with me only as something that was mine or that once qualified me. It is with me in that I love now as one who is reawakened, perhaps repentant and converted, in love.

So, then, within a committed relationship the meanings of the past and the future can change, yet something endures. It endures with intensity of life insofar as its past and its future, changing in ways subtle or dramatic, are nonetheless held together. The way open to us to sustain a living "presence" in a committed relationship, to make it whole without impoverishing it of its change and time, is the way of memory and hope. These are conditions for "presence," and they belong to the "way of fidelity."

RELAXATION OF HEART

The "way of fidelity" as I have described it thus far contains many paradoxes. It looks as if it would be travelled best by energetic action and choosing to pay attention, to do the deeds of love, to overcome inertia at every point. Perhaps it always requires "work," like the view of marriage which Barbara Ehrenreich describes as a "navigational feat that would have challenged a ballistics expert."[6] Concentrated activity, vigilance without respite, seems the order of our days.

There is another paradox within fidelity, however. If along its way we must summon strength to remain active participants and not mere observers, attentive seers and not just dreamers overwhelmed finally by our sleep, we must learn a relaxation of spirit which alone allows peak activity and peak receptivity. If we must "communicate," we must also learn to be silent; if we must "work at" our relationships, we must also learn to trust what we cannot manage or control.

The truth of this may be only a matter of common sense. We know, for example, that creative processes have power only insofar as they include both tension and relaxation, concentration and germination. We know, too, that if we are in anything "for the long run," it is necessary to "pace ourselves." And we know that there is a kind of "straining" that undermines our ability to love—whether it is straining for "perfection" (continually analyzing our motives, trying to outdo ourselves in deeds of love) or straining to make others be as we want them to be (or to protect them, or to please them). We know, then, that some form of inner relaxation is a necessary condition for sustaining our "presence" in long-term commitments to love.

Common sense, however, may not always reach as far as we need into the crises and opportunities of the "way of fidelity." "Relaxation of heart" can mean much more than "taking it easy" at key points along the way, much more even than one side of a rhythmic alternation of action and rest. Actually, I am using "relaxation" metaphorically to refer to a central element in the ongoing deep conversion of mind and heart needed for a great and truthful love. In this sense, it does not just prepare for peak activity and peak receptivity; it is part of it.

Perhaps the best way to portray relaxation of heart is to point to some examples of what it is and what it is not, where it appears and where it is missing. Thus, it is an aspect of the inner quality of commitment to a cause that yields steady zeal rather than fanaticism. It is part of the opening of one person to another that is the opposite of "hardening" one's heart, "stiffening" one's neck. It is the "letting go" of all one's objections and believing the word of another that we are really loved. Relaxation of heart characterizes the fearlessness that allows one to stop long enough to question an unexamined belief, and only thus to be able to enter deeply into that belief. It is the "melting" inside ourselves that permits a new revelation of beauty to transform the icy and forbidding reaches of our hearts.

"Relaxation" can be found in the center of "patience" when patience is strong enough to trust and wait for what "takes time." Relaxation of heart is the opposite of foolish patience (the toleration of injustices or stupidities that can and ought to be changed here and now). Rather, it is part of that patience which—while it is impatient for wholeness, for reason, for an end to irresponsibility—nonetheless refuses to close off in tightening bitterness. This kind of relaxation is not a "giving up" in premature surrender, not a sterile or cowardly resignation. It does not fear to name the nonsense or the unfairness that it must resist. Still, it waits even as it challenges; desires even as it trusts. It does not render anger impotent, but it keeps anger clear-sighted and keeps us free.

Irritation and impatience are such "small" emotions, but without a certain relaxation of heart they can defeat our greatest passions. Without being patient with ourselves as well as with those whom we choose to love, we are tempted to withdraw or to try to force a rhythm that does violence to the process of our commitment. There is, as Marcel saw, a "secret affinity between *hope* and relaxation."[7] And there is, as Etty Hillesum hints, that same affinity between relaxation and *desire*. "Our desire must be like a slow and stately ship, sailing across endless oceans, never in search of safe anchorage. Then suddenly, unexpectedly, it will find a mooring for a moment."[8] The power of this desire is not sustained by refusing commitment or by failing in fidelity; it is sustained by remaining present in hope— which is, in turn, sustained by the ability to relax one's heart.

We might think that to relax in any way would be to despair. We must, we say, "hold on" lest the bottom drop out of our commitment, lest our very selves fall apart. Paradoxically, however, there can be a kind of holding on too tightly and desperately against the fear of dissolution that becomes itself despair. To "let go," to stand alone before ourselves and those to whom we are committed, to consent to the pain "all the way inside"—this may be to discover that the bottom does not drop out, that we do not fall apart, that we are not, finally, alone. This letting-go, whether in joy or sorrow, whether in confrontation of myself or another, whether in wonder at or surrender to the truth of our relationship, is a kind of ultimate form of the "relaxation of heart" I am trying to portray. The "way of fidelity" can take a turn for us in which this becomes an ultimate condition for remaining "present." Even poets, however, only hint at such a meaning for relaxation of heart.

> O you tender ones. . . .
> Fear not suffering; the heaviness,
> give it back to the weight of the earth;
> the mountains are heavy, heavy the oceans.

> Even the trees you planted as children
> long since grew too heavy, you could not sustain them.
> Ah, but the breezes . . . ah, but the spaces. . . .[9]

CO-PRESENCE

I have not spoken, except indirectly, about mutuality in our relationships of committed love. That is, I have talked about the "way of fidelity" almost as if it were travelled by means of "my" decisions only, my imagination and memory, my strength alone. Fidelity might seem, then, a rather private and individual matter, though obviously with consequences for more persons than myself. In such a view, we perhaps take account of the concrete reality of those to whom we are committed, but we count on ourselves alone.

This, however, is not what I have meant to imply. Every commitment to persons involves some form of mutuality. After all, I give my word *to someone*—to someone who receives it, who holds it, who makes a claim on me. Even if I am committed to someone who does not know about my commitment (for example, to a comatose patient or an oblivious people), or if I am committed to someone who refuses to accept my *promise* (for example, a rebellious child), there is still a sense in which I experience "mutuality." Something in the other binds me to her or him, calls to me, makes it easier or more difficult for me to be faithful, and places in sharp relief the painfulness of the forms of mutuality that are missing.

I want to focus now, however, on the more ordinary meaning of mutuality in commitments—that is, on commitments that are mutually made. Here there is mutual giving and receiving of the words of commitment; here there is a shared responsibility for traversing the "way of fidelity." Two liberties meet. Two experiences of time in some way intersect. Two life-processes are somehow shared.

Unfortunately, the rhetoric we use to describe mutual love and commitment too often exceeds the reality of our experience. Human longing for friendship, for companionship, for shared passion makes us think that if only a *mutual* commitment to love can be managed, we shall more easily be faithful. But mutuality itself becomes a struggle, and the challenges to fidelity multiply. Within mutual commitments there can be "worlds of pain," the term used by author Lillian Rubin for family life in the working class in this country (but a term that could cross many a class and many a form of relationship). A glimpse into these worlds shows them not to be unique.

> I'm not sure what I want. I keep talking to him about communication, and he says, "Okay, so we're talking; now what do you want?" And I don't know what to say then, but I know that's not what I mean.

> I swear, I don't know what she wants. She keeps saying we have to talk, and then when we do, it always turns out I'm saying the wrong thing.[10]

The same kind of world, across time and space, produces tragedy in Sigrid Undset's trilogy about Kristin Lavransdatter:

> She clenched her teeth in the dark. Never would she beg and beseech—if he chose to be silent, she would be silent, too. . . . Bitterness surged in her heart; but she lay stock-still against the wall. . . .

She was hot and hard with wrath—she grew wild with rage when she marked that he would look searchingly at her and then hastily look away. . . .

"Yet had I not believed of you, Kristin, that you could go about thus, bearing a hidden grudge against me, and yet seeming kind and joyous as ever."[11]

Why should it be so difficult to sustain a mutual commitment to love and to share a life? Why should it be so painful to be faithful when we have the added support of someone else's responding love?

Here lies the great mystery of the countless forms of our inability to blend our lives together. It is here that we begin to see the vast chasms that sometimes lie between us and another person or group of persons. "Men and women are infinitely ingenious in their ability to find ways of being unhappy together."[12] We who take slogan words like "complementarity" for granted find that the more usual course turns out to be trying to overcome incompatibility. It does not matter if it is men and women together who encounter such great difficulty (though it may be more intractable for them), or whole families of persons, or friends of whatever gender, or coworkers. The mountains to be crossed between us all too often appear when we try to meet each other in the depths of our lives—to meet not just for a glorious moment of union, but in order to share whole lives.

I am not talking only of the fears we may encounter—fears of rejection on the one hand and of being consumed by another person on the other. I am not talking only of those strange demons that come seemingly from nowhere, like jealousy, envy, general hostility, possessiveness, self-pity, or a hankering for constant affirmation. Nor am I talking just of the deprivations in our individual psychological histories or our manifold ignorance of much of what constitutes the human person. And I do not speak only of social impoverishments that render us unprepared for the challenges of mutuality, incapable of respect for every person, not always up to honesty or humility or courage. I am talking, in addition to such things (and perhaps above all), of the myriad small incapacities within us for mutuality in relationship. It does not take satanic pride or severe pathology to miss the crucial moves in the process of mutual love or to hurt those we ordinarily want to affirm.

In our efforts at mutuality it is as if the general problems of fidelity escalate and are prone to exaggeration. The obstacles I confront in myself are doubled by the obstacles in you, and the difficulties I produce can be reinforced by the response they elicit from you. The problems of impatience, of weariness, distraction, the vicissitudes of feeling, conflicts in desire, the waxing and waning of love—all the problems we have already seen besetting fidelity in any case are potentially greater, not less, in commitments to mutual love. "Little things leave the greatest scars," and there are more of them when they are between us. Two hardening hearts make love more remote; and the injury one inflicts on the other wounds more deeply, perhaps because our expectation is for something so much better.

Of course, it is necessary here as in other forms of commitment to try to understand the obstacles to mutuality, starting with one's own and one's partner's limitations and weaknesses, tendencies to evil, and indifference. It is necessary as well to try to understand each one's strengths and unique potential for goodness and truth. And we need to understand simply the differences between us—differences that are neither good nor bad, not particular limitations or extraordinary capacities for greatness—just differences. While we try to understand all of this, however, the "conditions of presence" that are essential for fidelity to persons in general become, if this is possible, even more crucial for fidelity to mutual love.

We cannot sustain presence to one another without memory and hope and "relaxation of heart." Without a willingness to learn how to remember and so to hope, how to relax our hearts, we will not grow in mutual presence. Today we readily acknowledge the essential requirement of "communication" for the sharing of lives and the protection as well as the nurturance of mutual love. Communication is important, however, because it gives us access not only to each one's static present but to a "field of presence." Through communication we enter one another's life and time, one another's memory and hope. In it we may gain a common memory and share a common hope. And the freedom we need for this requires relaxation of heart.

I may be overdramatizing the difficulties of mutual fidelity. It is also true that mutuality offers, by reason of what it is, an *aid* to fidelity. After all, I can be helped in my attention to what I love by the active reminder of a partner. The continuity of my love can be saved by the forgiveness of my beloved. My engagement in my commitment is strengthened by a mutual bond. I am less likely to become "unhitched" from my commitment if it is not only up to me to overcome inertia, and if I am actively called back from the temptation to become a spectator. Even when the participation in my commitment is painful, marked by bitter confrontation or misunderstanding, I can by that very pain be kept alive (keeping in mind, of course, that it is sentimental nonsense to claim that every such pain is a source of life).

There are other ways that mutuality of commitment serves our efforts to be faithful. *Any* commitment, whether in itself mutual or not, is more easily kept when there is some kind of *community* context and support, when what Margaret Miles calls the "weight of the individual's primary longing and commitment" is distributed beyond the focal point of a single personal relationship.[13] This can mean a number of things, including that we are upheld in our otherwise fragile commitments by the very fact that others (whether a family or a network of friends or a church or a voluntary association) know about these commitments and share them with us. We are importantly carried by the momentum of the activity of others. We are confirmed in our intentions by the ability of others to ease our doubts. Our memories make more sense when they are rooted in the story of a people or group. Our hopes seem more real when we see them shining from the hearts of others whom we love and respect. Our seriousness is tempered by a community's recurring humor and play. Our foolishness is balanced by a communal sense of purpose. We can afford the risks of both greater joy and suffering when they are never ours alone.

Of course, community support of commitments in this sense can be dangerous as well as helpful. We can hide within its safety, forget to examine our commitments because of its complacency. We can be carried forward with a fervor that is blind, a fanaticism that arms us with passion and moves us to crusades of destruction. We can help to build myths that cover injustice and fail to see the need to discern the "way of fidelity" not only for ourselves but for our community. What can truly aid the best of our commitments can also undermine them or seduce us into other commitments that are harmful to ourselves and to others. Still, what is dangerous in this regard is so because of its potential power for nourishing and sustaining our presence within our commitments.

So community can help us to understand better the bonds between us; it can remind us to attend to one another and to care for our love. Paradoxically, it can also *serve* our mutual commitment by turning us *away from* a focus solely on our mutual, communal relationship. When our only concern is the commitment we have made to one another (whether we are many or only two), our lives become constricted. We expect too much from this one union, place too much weight on hopes that rely only on it. More importantly, we miss the truth that we are made not only for union but for more and more inclusive, universal union. We may even miss learning of the possibility of such a truth.

Here is another paradox. It is essential for us to attend to our own mutual relationship, to care for it in caring for one another. Yet it is also essential to turn away from ourselves and to focus together on something beyond us—something in relation to which we may undertake a commitment. We can hold what we together love (that is other than ourselves) within the bond that is already between us. And the bond between us may thereby be enhanced and made secure.

But the paradox does not end here. For it may be that the bond between us is enhanced by our shared relationship with someone or something beyond ourselves *only to the extent* that we do not make of this new relationship a mere *means* to our own union. Our bond deepens in this way only when we turn to something beyond us because it is important in itself; only when we do not commit ourselves to still others (even our own children, for example) merely as instruments for the preservation of our own union, but instead because they are valuable in themselves.

This is what many call commitment to a "third," to something larger than ourselves, in relation to which we share choices, concerns, responsibilities, and hence mutual enlargement of heart. Barbara Ehrenreich points to an example of this when she speculates that we "might meet as rebels together—not against each other but against a social order that condemns so many of us. . . . If we can do this, if we can make a *common* commitment to ourselves and future generations, then it may also be possible to rebuild the notion of *personal* commitment. . . ."[14]

Finally, it would be a mistake to overlook one more way in which mutual commitments to mutual love constitute a special part of the "way of fidelity." Mutuality, when it is right and good, partakes of the goal of human life in a way that makes it precisely as mutual a source of strength for whatever other means we must take to be faithful to it. Human love can be great and wise when it is faithful to friends and partners who forget us, or to enemies who betray us and oppose all that we hold dear. Indeed, the truest (or at least the purest) loves we achieve in this life may be of such a kind—that is, precisely not mutual. "Therefore, I say to you, love your enemies" (Matt. 5:45). Yet the fullness of love, and hence the goal of love, is in communion—in loving and being loved, knowing and being known—and finally in the sustained communion that has traditionally been called "friendship," a mutually committed love and sharing of life. It is this to which the "way of fidelity" leads. But our very inklings of this (along our way and not just at the end of it) are healing; for they are sources of peace, and harbingers that give direction to hope.

Does all of this leave us with anything to help the "cases" I mentioned elsewhere? Henry, in his longing for renewed life in family and job? Or Sheila, in her quandary over options of divorce or a transformed relationship with her husband? Or Karen, in her experience of the silence of God? Rachel, in her puzzlement over the limitations of her profession? As I have forewarned, no list of "how to's" can finally answer their questions or ease their life situations. Yet there *are* markers which *can* help them, or any of us, to find and to go along the "way of fidelity."

It may not be enough for Henry to decide to believe in his "original vision," nor enough for him to remember the history of his love. It may be insufficient for him to look up and try to see again or catch a new glimpse of purpose in his work, new meaning in his life, a new ground of respect for his wife and children. It may not change everything for him to use his imagination to probe the future for possibilities in which he can hope, which he can help to bring about. It may not renew his life to "relax his heart" and listen for, invent, risk new forms of mutuality in his relationships. None of these things may be sufficient in themselves to remedy his situation, and the "way of fidelity" may be lost for him (or doomed to be a completely barren way). But *without* them—without decisions to believe, and without memory and hope, relaxation of heart, an understanding of mutuality—he will surely lose the way. With them, he may find it.

The same is true, I would argue, for Rachel and Sheila and Karen, or for any of us. Insights into fidelity, the nature of its "way" and the conditions that help us in it, are not enough to solve all of our difficulties or carry us along with surety. But they yield more than trite sayings. For *without* these insights (in however reflective or unre-flective a form) our chances of being faithful are very small.

Who knows, of course, what unexpected graces may come to us to do what is otherwise impossible? Who can deny that powers of fidelity are sometimes born in us unawares? But if we look closely, we may see that "grace" *knows* the "way of fidelity"; that what is graced *in* us is our memory and our hope, our power to discern and to choose, our courage to believe in the original promise, our capacity to relax our hearts and so to "rise up to meet the dawn." What grace works *among* us is a growing solidarity, and *between us* a capacity for intimacy. Whether we think that we struggle every inch of the way by ourselves, or that we are overwhelmed by an empowering grace, or that here above all "two liberties meet," human and divine—the "way of fidelity" is made possible by "conditions of presence."

It remains for us to ask whether in every commitment fidelity is possible, and whether for every commitment fidelity is obligated.

Chapter 6

Discerning Obligation: Can There Be Release?

The next two chapters, insofar as they are successful in their aim, will disappoint some who read them. While it is here that I come finally to questions of obligation (questions that I have more than once put off in previous chapters), it is also here that the difficulty of providing general answers for every specific problem of the binding power of commitment is most evident.

The questions are the questions of Stephen and Ann, of Harriet, of Sheila, of anyone or any group still asking: Ought we to keep the promises we have made? Must we keep them, no matter what? Does the fact that a relationship is experienced as destructive justify its being left behind? What if it is only not "fulfilling"? If we find that we cannot be equally faithful to all of the commitments we have made, how do we determine which ones have priority in their claim on us? What is the role of "duty" in our struggles for "fidelity"? How do we weigh the importance of our own needs in relation to the needs of others for whom we have promised to care? Can there be obligations to break or to change commitments, as well as obligations to keep them?

PERSPECTIVE

Before I try to address these kinds of questions directly, it is perhaps only fair that I indicate something of the perspective from which I shall be considering what are, after all, controversial issues. A few preliminary statements in this regard will not justify my approach, but they will help to explain it; and, above all, they will help to "locate" it so that those who wish to consider other approaches may do so. Six such statements should suffice.

1. The way that I shall take in exploring the nature and extent of obligations undertaken by commitments is a way that requires some tolerance for ambiguity. Discernment of the "right thing to do" regarding profound human commitments can be troublingly difficult whether one experiences the commitment from within (as one of the parties to it) or from without (as an "impartial" observer). There are, in my view, no easy formulas for determining whether or not we ought to keep certain commitments. Two positions could be adopted that would make it much easier, of course. We could hold, on the one hand, that every promise binds absolutely, that there are no circumstances, no consequences, no conditions that justify breaking a promise once it is made. Or, on the other hand, we could hold that there is nothing intrinsic to a promise such that by itself it binds us to fulfill it; that the obligation to keep promises, like all other obligations, is wholly relative to an overarching obligation to bring about the best possible consequences of our actions. Given this view, if some important good can come from breaking a promise, then we ought simply and always to break it.

Either of these two positions might solve, for example, Sheila's question of whether or not she should begin divorce proceedings against her husband, Joshua. If she adopts the first position, she clearly ought not to try to end her marriage (for her marriage vows hold "no matter what"). If she adopts the second position, she may judge that nothing binds her to Joshua once she concludes that she and the children can be happier apart from him and that no great social harm will come from her leaving him. Though he may ask her to keep her word to him, this has no weight in the balance of goods that she believes can come from their divorce.

Yet even these two seemingly clear-cut positions cannot always solve our problems of commitment. For one thing, we may vacillate between the positions, unable to rest finally convinced that either one by itself is morally adequate in the face of our disrupted lives. Or, even if we are convinced that all promises absolutely should be kept, there often remains the question of what we really intended when we promised. No new stipulations of conditions may change our obligation, but what were the implicit conditions built into the promise in the first place? If, on the other hand, we are confident that the obligation to keep our word always collapses before circumstances where harm will be done by fulfilling our promise, there often remain the difficult questions of how much harm and to whom, or how much good and whose good in relation to whose harm.

In any case, I do not in these chapters adopt either of these extreme positions. I want neither to absolutize the obligation to keep our commitments nor to relativize it out of existence in favor of a general obligation to avoid harmful consequences or produce good ones. I shall treat it as a real and serious obligation, but one among many moral obligations in our lives, some of which may take priority over the obligation to fulfill a specific commitment.

2. To say that we are not able to settle all questions of concrete obligation to commitments "ahead of time" does not mean that we are bereft of common insights regarding such obligations. We need not struggle in our decisions alone, as if each situation were totally unique and resolvable only in an ad hoc way. There *are* general guidelines or general considerations to be taken into account, which we can find when we engage in common analysis of even the most difficult situations. This is especially important today when in our culture we appear to be faced by a multitude of problems and immense suffering in committed relationships, some of which need to be thought through by all of us in a systematic way. There is, in other words, some wisdom to be gained and shared among us.

3. Moral theorists who try to test the meaning and degree of our obligations to keep promises tend to look at extreme cases like that of a promise made to someone on her deathbed (a case in which the "claim" that I give to another cannot be exercised in the obvious ways). While such cases have merit for illuminating the whole human practice of promise-making, they do not help all that much in resolving the kinds of relational problems that recur so often in ordinary people's lives. Hence, the kind of case I want to keep before us is the kind that occurs, especially today, in almost everyone's life—cases like those of Stephen and Ann, of Karen, of

Jack and Beth, of Henry and Sheila and Harriet. With such cases, too, I want to continue to focus on the "prime case" of commitment, an interpersonal commitment to love, though I shall not restrict my concern only to this.

4. There is a twofold danger in trying to articulate the nature and extent of obligations to commitments. One is the danger of abetting our tendencies to scrupulosity and moral rigidity; we can escalate the seeming power of promises so that we are not free even to consider the possibility of needed change in our lives. The other danger, however, is that of weakening our sense of obligation to commitments, aiding our tendencies and refining our skills for rationalization. In order to limit both of these risks, it is helpful to remember the questions not only of those who consider keeping or breaking commitments, but of those who have been recipients of commitments. The picture of obligation (especially when it is explicitly reciprocal) will not be complete if we ask only whether I should be faithful to you and not also whether you should be faithful to me.

5. The heart of the question before us at this point is the moral obligation, or "duty," that arises precisely because we have made a commitment. It is not all the other reasons we may have for keeping our commitments. There *are* other reasons, of course. There is the love that prompted the commitment, a love that now somehow *is morally obligated* (by the promise) but that can also, now as in the beginning, be spontaneous. It is this love that I have considered in the previous two chapters dealing with fidelity and to which I shall have to return in order to understand the interplay between love and obligation. This love may prove to be of ultimate importance in determining the nature of my obligation; it may also be obligated for reasons other than the fact that I have promised it.

There are other reasons, too, for keeping commitments. The sociologist Howard Becker called them "side bets."[1] These are factors in addition to the central point of a commitment (besides, for example, the love or the deeds of love that are promised, and besides the moral obligation that the promise itself entails), factors that nonetheless hold us in our commitments. These may be things like security, or just being "used to" a situation, or financial losses that would be incurred if we moved out of a commitment. Thus, for example, a woman might be motivated to stay with a certain job, not only because she was morally committed to it, but because a change would mean loss of her pension, or the upset of her household if she had to move, or the need to learn new skills if she looked for another position, and so on.

These kinds of "side bets" can be extremely important in our decisions to remain in a committed relationship. They constitute part of the "stake" we have in the commitment, part of what we have yielded (even if only by letting them accumulate in this commitment-relation rather than another) and stand to lose if we break the commitment. They may even have moral weight in the decision if they involve some kind of good or harm for ourselves or for others. But insofar as they do not constitute a moral claim on us precisely because of the commitment itself (the categorical claim to be faithful to our word because we have pledged it), they are not the precise matter for consideration in this chapter. Here, rather, my central concern is the content and basis of the moral obligation entailed by commitment itself.

6. In my view, the fundamental question for our obligations to faithfulness is the question of a "just" love. This sounds esoteric, perhaps, but I mean it to be eminently practical, as close as possible to the concrete demands rising out of our commitment relationships. To speak of a "just love" may also sound as if I am short-circuiting the whole issue of promise-keeping, blurring it under a general and unspecified obligation to love. The meaning of a "just" love and its relevance for commitment-obligations will have to be made clear as I go along. In my view, nothing is more critical, however, for sorting out competing claims and responsibilities, for understanding our obligations to individuals and to a common good, and for discerning our obligations of faithfulness to others and to ourselves.

THE OBLIGATION

The fact that a moral obligation follows from my making a commitment to another person or persons should be evident if the meaning I have been giving all along to commitment is accepted. I have described commitment, indeed, as the *yielding of a claim* to another— the yielding of a moral claim over some future actions of mine. Thus, if we ask why I "ought" to keep my commitments, the first and most obvious answer is that this is what commitment *means*; what commitment *does* is produce an "ought." It effects a form of relationship in which I am morally bound (not physically, not just legally, not just in terms of pragmatic considerations, but *morally* bound) to keep my word—to act in accordance with the word I have given. By a commitment I "undertake" a moral obligation.[2]

Suppose we introduce traditional moral language to describe the obligation entailed by commitment. Then we might speak in the following ways: If I, in and through commitment, give someone a claim over me, then it is a matter of "justice" that I honor the claim (according to the limits of the commitment). Something now is "due" that person. What I have given to her is a new "right" in relation to me. If I fail to give what is thereby due, I "violate" her right (unless my failure can be "justified" in some way). I contradict something that now is constitutive of the relationship between us. In "breaking faith," I "break my word," and so break, contradict, my own integrity as a person. I wrong the other person, failing to acknowledge the true claim that is hers. I do a kind of violence to the bond between us. The same, of course, is true the other way around—when someone without justification breaks her or his word to me.

Part of the reason I can be said to wrong someone when I betray my word to him is that I thereby restrict his options in a way that can be called coercive in his regard. That is, if he has been led by me to believe that he can count on whatever I have promised, he will make his choices on that basis. If this trust proves unfounded, his choices will have been unjustifiably limited.

The basis of our obligation to keep commitments can be described more broadly than this, however.[3] When we fail to be faithful to our promises, we not only *wrong* one another as persons; we can truly *harm* each other and many others beyond us. This is the central concern of those who argue that promises must be kept because of the bad consequences that follow from breaking them. "Harm" may take many forms, but there is one that is always a possibility when a commitment is broken. That is, commitments provide a basis of trust in our relationships, whether they are with individuals or are broadly communal and social. To the extent that commitments are ignored or broken without clearly justifying reasons, trust is eroded. When we fail to keep a promise, those who counted on us may lose faith not only in us but in all others who seek their trust. They may experience themselves (as I have already noted) as exploited, used, deceived, as coerced or abandoned because their own choices were made in the light of their earlier trust in our promises to them. As a result, alienation, resentment, suspicion can enter in. Moreover, we who break our promises may find ourselves becoming the kind of persons who are more and more irresponsible as we attend less and less to the conditions of accountability. Less responsible (that is, more irresponsible), we are paradoxically less free to enter into human relationships, less free to collaborate in human endeavors.

Beyond its importance for individuals, there is general acknowledgment that promise-keeping is one of the foundations of society. When it is commonly expected that promises will not be kept, people lose their moorings, and society staggers into chaos, often on the brink of violence. There is, in other words, an "institutional" consequence when promises are taken lightly, and this alone is serious enough to sustain a rule of promise-keeping.

Despite all of this, very few of us would insist that the obligation entailed by commitments is absolute. Common sense has taught us that some promises should, in fact, *not* be kept. Those who theorize about such matters (though usually arguing strongly in support of the rule of promise-keeping) have tried to express for us the moral "logic" of why the rule of promise-keeping does not always hold. Or they have tried to show us that moral logic itself must be subordinated to the overall "narrative," or "story," of our lives; and that in the context of our stories it can become clear that not all commitments are to be kept. Theorizing like this to any great extent may seem superfluous to many people who struggle with their own commitments. It is sometimes criticized for obscuring the importance of "persons" by entangling us with abstract "principles" (or the opposite, obscuring the force of principles by veiling them in contexts and stories). My own conviction, however, is that all of these considerations constitute an important part of our collectible wisdom. Taking account of them can at the very least provoke our own thinking and aid our own efforts to discern what, in a given situation, we ought to do.

RELEASE FROM OBLIGATION

Among the philosophers and theologians with whom we can converse on these matters, we need not turn only to our contemporaries. Ancient, medieval, and modern thinkers affirmed the obligation of promise-keeping, but they also struggled with questions of the limits of that obligation. Cicero, for example, in the first century B.C.E. offered the view that promises are not binding when keeping them would jeopardize someone's life or health or even reputation.[4] He described one case in which a man was given medicine for dropsy on the condition that, should he be cured, he would never use the medicine again. The man was cured, but became ill with the same disease a second time. Cicero thought that, in this case, the man was not bound to his earlier promise never to take the medicine again. In another example, Cicero described a situation in which a rich man left money to a wise man but in doing so exacted the promise that, after his death, the wise man would dance in the public square. Cicero commented that if the wise man believed it would be morally wrong for him to dance publicly, he could (on facing his conscience later, after the rich man's death) break his promise. Cicero thought he should then, however, refuse the money (unless he contributed it to the state to help in a "grave crisis"—in which case he could dance or not, as he saw fit)! However quaint such examples seem to us, they suggest at least the possibility of finding reasonable grounds for not keeping some commitments.

In the thirteenth century Thomas Aquinas tried to identify when the obligation of commitments (especially vows made to God) could be released. While some commitments in his view could never be granted a dispensation (that is, their obligation released), others might be. Among the latter were vows made to do something that was evil (an action that was evil in itself or in its consequences), or useless, or an impediment to a greater good.[5] Medieval theologians like Aquinas also thought that vows might be released if they became impossible to fulfill (a favorite example being the impossibility of fulfilling a vow to make a pilgrimage to a shrine if the shrine was destroyed before one could get to it).

Even Immanuel Kant, the philosopher most often cited as the upholder of absolute moral duties, did not treat the obligation to keep promises as strictly as he did the obligation to tell the truth. (What Kant did prohibit absolutely were "lying promises"—that is, promises made deceptively, with the express intention of not keeping them.)[6] In his larger theory he allowed, for example, friendships (at least friendships of "taste") to come to an end (if "we fail to find what we imputed to our friend and sought in him"), though "we must still reverence the old friendship and never show that we are capable of hate."[7] Contracts, too, might be modified according to "equity," so that the letter of the law of the original contract would not be binding in a "strict" sense, but accommodated to changed circumstances.[8]

When we turn to contemporary writers we find general agreement that *some* justifying reasons can release us from otherwise binding commitments. This, however, can have very different meanings, and there is strong disagreement on whether and how commitments do not bind. For example, Richard McCormick argues that "the inherent goodness (and therefore meaning) of a promise is *a limited* goodness and may concur with a more urgent value demanding value preference."[9] Paul Ramsey, opposing exceptions to rules like promise-keeping (and insisting on the stringency of "faithfulness" requirements of Christian commitments), allows room for *specifying* rules so that limiting conditions can at least be built into the original meaning of a commitment.[10] And A. I. Melden, arguing all the while that "Admittedly one ought to keep one's promises," nonetheless adds: "But this does not settle the question whether, here and now, in such-and-such circumstances, one ought . . . to keep one's promise. For it may be the better part of moral wisdom to break one's promise in order to help a stranger in need, or, in quite different circumstances, to turn away from someone in need in order to keep one's word."[11]

Commitments, of course, even interpersonal ones, are of greatly varying degrees of significance in our lives. It is difficult to talk in the same breath of the obligations involved in a promise to join some acquaintances for a picnic and the obligations entailed by a marriage vow. The British philosopher Elizabeth Anscombe points to this when she cautions:"I should perhaps say here that I don't take an enormously strenuous view of the obligation created by the mere fact of having given an undertaking to do something. There are many cases of undertakings from the obligation of which a mere small degree of inconvenience exempts us. . . . [S]olemn commitments are comparative rarities, though they tend to be prominent when they occur."[12] Not everyone would take as lightly as Anscombe the balancing of inconvenience with the obligation to keep promises, but it is surely clear that our real problems are with the "solemn commitments."

My own position is that all valid commitments obligate us by reason of what commitment itself means. Yet this obligation sometimes does not "hold." When and why does it not hold? If we scan the traditions of moral philosophy and theology (as well as, I believe, the ordinary experience of persons who face these questions in their own lives), we find a fairly common set of considerations that offer likely reasons for releasing an obligation to keep one's commitment or promise. Most of these can be included under the following four categories.

1. *The Original Meaning of the Commitment.* Our original intentions, capabilities, and processes in making a commitment can become the basis for a later judgment that the commitment does not obligate us to its fulfillment. It may be that there was no real commitment in the first place or that the commitment that did exist was circumscribed in a way that now releases us from our obligation.

But if the words of commitment were once spoken (or the symbols exchanged, the forms signed, the role accepted, and so forth), how can there not have been a commitment "in the first place"? Just as there are minimum requirements for the validity of legal contracts, so there are minimum requirements for any promise, any commitment, actually to be made. The *one making it*, for example, must have the *capacities* ordinarily required for free choice—hence, not be too young, or mentally incompetent; not be coerced by force or fear or fraud; not be seduced in a way that makes the assignment of responsibility unreasonable; and not be ignorant of factors that essentially change the nature of the commitment-relation.

Moreover, the validity of a commitment depends on certain requirements regarding its *matter* and *the way it is made*. It is generally believed, for example, that commitments cannot be made (in a way that effects obligation) to do things that are immoral, or that are unwanted by the recipient of the commitment, or that are foolish (trivial, or foolhardy in that they demand a sacrifice wholly disproportionate to the value to be gained). "Vows about vain and useless things should be ridiculed rather than respected."[13] Some commitments do not bind "in the first place" because they conflict with prior commitments (as, for example, when a marriage is thought to be invalid because it is bigamous). And if a commitment is meant to be mutual, some degree of mutual understanding of what is being promised, and mutual acceptance of the promises, is required.

When a commitment is successfully made, and an obligation is thereby undertaken, it binds only within the *limits of its making*.[14] Most commitments are conditional (again, "in the first place") in some way. That is, they are intended to be binding only if or when or as long as certain conditions are met. In fact, some theorists (as we have seen) would argue that "exceptions" to the obligation of keeping a commitment are really only clarifications of its original meaning. For example, if a woman decides to divorce her husband because he continues to use physical violence against her, it could be argued that implicit in the marriage agreement was the condition that she would not be beaten.[15]

2. *Release by the Promisee.* Because the obligation to keep a commitment comes from yielding to someone a claim over me, it follows that if the claim is waived or relinquished by the recipient, my obligation ceases. Thus, if I promised to bring my friend a book, and he phones me to say that he no longer wants it, it is silly to think that I am still obligated to bring it to him. It is not a question of

breaking my commitment; the claim is simply dropped. So, too, the claim in a mutual commitment might be simply mutually dropped.

3. *Impossibility of Fulfillment.* If one accepts the Kantian principle that "ought implies can," the fact that it becomes impossible to fulfill a commitment should lead to the conclusion that one's obligation in this case does not hold. Charles Fried points to the relevance of this consideration in contract law, citing the paradigm case of *Taylor v. Caldwell.* The owner of a music hall had contracted with a group of performers for their use of the hall on a certain day. In the meantime, the hall burned down. Though the question of liability in such a case may not be simple, legal relief was granted on the grounds of the literal impossibility of fulfillment of the contract.[16]

4. *Competing Obligations.* As I have already indicated, the principle of promise-keeping is not an absolute principle in the sense that it can never be overridden by another moral principle, such as "Do no injury." As the philosopher A. I. Melden puts it, "it is manifestly absurd to suppose that promising . . . always takes precedence over . . . truth-telling, life-saving, parent or children-caring, or whatever."[17] The claim I have given to someone by my promise always points in the direction of an obligation, but other claims (even claims from other commitments) may actually determine a different obligation in a given situation. For example, ongoing duties of friendship may conflict with claims on my time arising from professional commitments. Or it may happen that keeping a commitment will entail serious harm to the promisee, or to others, or to myself. In such a situation, the obligation not to harm persons (even myself) may take priority over the obligation to keep a promise.

Though they may finally be inadequate by themselves, these four categories do offer seemingly straightforward possibilities for determining when a commitment no longer holds. A little reflection on them, however, shows quickly just how difficult it is to apply even these as measures of commitment-obligation. For example, it seems fairly simple to evaluate the *original circumstances and limitations* of a commitment and to find there, if possible, reasons that justify release from obligation. Most of our commitments, however, are not made with the precision of purely legal contracts. It is one thing to declare a contract invalid because it was made by a minor (or even to wade through the legal complexities involved in determining mental competency); it is quite another to determine whether a marriage or a religious vow was undertaken when one was psychologically not mature enough to assume so serious a commitment. It is also one thing to determine default regarding an explicitly stipulated condition in a lease for an apartment; it is another thing altogether to achieve clarity regarding what were only implicit but finally nonnegotiable boundaries for acceptable action on the part of one's spouse (for example, did one really include in a marital commitment the implicit condition "as long as I shall not be physically abused"?).

Moreover, it is not always the case that we remain unbound by foolish promises. Nor is it the case that a prior obligation (which should perhaps constitute an impediment to a new, conflicting commitment) always in fact prevents a new obligation from arising. Most of us know intuitively the truth of the central dilemma in Graham Greene's *The Heart of the Matter.* Potential tragedy lurks in Major Scobie's wry and painful recognition that in beginning an extramarital affair he has undertaken an obligation—even though it contradicts his obligation to his wife. "He had sworn to preserve Louise's happiness and now he had accepted another and contradictory responsibility."[18]

Even the notion of being *released from a promise by the promisee* is not as simple as it first appears. There are commitments in which the new wishes of the recipient do not seem to make the commitment evaporate. Suppose, for example, that I have promised to love someone who then rejects my love and my promise. I may have to remove myself from active contact with this person, but it is possible that I do not consider myself at all released from my commitment and that the commitment-relation is not dissolved. Even though all I can do is to respect lovingly the wishes of the other to place physical distance between us, this in itself may be my way of being faithful to my commitment. Kierkegaard says of this occurrence in a friendship: "Imagine a compound word which lacks the last word; there is only the first word and the hyphen (for the one who breaks the relationship still cannot take the hyphen with him; the lover naturally keeps the hyphen on his side)."[19] The same is undoubtedly true in commitment-relationships like those between family members, especially between parents and children.[20]

Nor is it a simple matter to discern when it is *impossible to fulfill* a commitment. For in interpersonal commitments "possibility" and "impossibility" are not readily distinguished. What is most often in question is not sheer physical possibility but psychological (or spiritual or moral) possibility; and it is often not a question of only one person's capacity but of the capacities of whoever shares the commitment-relationship. In addition, when one aspect of what has been promised cannot be sustained, it may still be that *something* is possible (and thereby obligated). One may be, as Thomas Aquinas insisted, obligated at least to be "ready to do what one can."[21]

When it comes to *competing obligations* (not original impedi-ments to a commitment, but those conflicts between obligations that arise inevitably in the complicated living out of our lives), only a clear hierarchical ordering of principles and commitments can make the resolution of conflicts among them a simple matter. But no consensus on such ordering is available in traditional wisdom, and we know the complexities of our experience too well to hope that we can fashion one that will remove all doubt about our obligations. Some ordering, of course, is possible, and some method of resolving conflicts is necessary. St. Augustine, for example, when reproached by his friends for his neglect of them in favor of other members of his congregation, professed a principle of priority that made *need* the determining factor. "Charity, like a nurse caring for her children, gives the weak preference over the strong, not that they are more worthy of love, but more needy of help, and she wishes them to be like the others whom she passes over for a time as a mark of trust, not contempt."[22]

Others, however, have argued that the closeness of our relationships with persons (our "proximity" to them) is the determinant of priority of claim; thus, claims by members of our family would take priority over claims made on us by others. Given this view, it might be argued that commitment-obligations take priority over general demands to care for the well-being of those in greatest need. We are, in all of these considerations, thrown back to our earlier questions of how great a need, how close a relationship, how great a help or harm, how important the commitment to the one who receives it, how many persons will be aided or injured, and so on. The process of balancing claims is not avoided, though it is helped, by an appeal to an order of principles.

Finally, perhaps none of the four categories addresses directly the reason most often given for breaking a commitment: Things simply have changed since the time when the commitment was made. I have changed and you have changed, and the relationship between us has changed. The original reason for the commitment is gone, though it can hardly be argued that this was foreseen and provided for in the original implicit or explicit limits of the obligation. It is not that it is impossible to keep the commitment, but it no longer makes sense to keep it at the price of ignoring the changes between us. We might both relinquish the claim we have on each other and remove the obligation in that way. But suppose one of us does not want to do that or, even if we both are agreed, we have no way of soliciting agreement from the wider community with whom we shared our commitment. Perhaps it is a matter of competing moral claims, but perhaps it is, rather, a matter of a claim competing with a great desire. The point of the commitment, of course, was to bind us together in spite of and through the changes that would come. But can it now hold, can it now really obligate, in the face of all that has happened?

This question, along with the difficulties of applying the previous four categories, prompts me to try another approach to the overall issue of the continuing duty involved in commitment. I come then to what I have called the fundamental question of a "just love." Within it, the categories of original meaning, relinquishment of the claim by the recipient, impossibility of fulfillment of the commitment, and competing obligations, will not be left behind. But other considerations must be added to them and some interpretive keys provided.

Chapter 7

Discerning Obligation: A Just Love

Once again, to commit ourselves to love someone is to give a law to our love. It is to give a new claim, to undertake a new level of obligation, for loving and for a way of loving according to the content of our commitment. If we are ever to be justified in breaking such a commitment, what must be justified is some change in our love or our way of expressing it. But can we ever be truly released from an obligation to love? or from a framework in which we have pledged to live out our love? Can the "law" of our commitment either no longer bind our love, or can it come into so great a conflict with our love that love itself abrogates the law we have given it? These are crucial questions for "duty" and for love. They are not the only questions, however, for on the "other side" of them lies the positive question: How am I still bound? The questions beg for a return to a consideration of love itself, and to some understanding of its intrinsic norms.

A JUST LOVE

The description of love that I adopted in chapter 3, and which I have assumed throughout, is that of an affective affirmation that is responsive and unitive. By and in our love we affirm, "I want you to be and to be firm and full in being." The essential sign of my love is that I do the deeds of love insofar as they are called for and possible. With only this description, however, it seems that we can love wisely or foolishly, with an evil love or a good one, an unjust or just, destructive or creative love. Sometimes we talk as if foolish loves, or evil and destructive loves, are not real loves. Yet surely they can be affective, unitive, and in some sense affirmative responses.

A father or mother, for example, may love a child primarily as a duplication of or a projection of themselves. In this love they may be extremely attentive to the child, meeting his every wish, but pushing him to a future that will ultimately be destructive to him. Shall we call this love? Or the owner of a large manufacturing company cares for her workers in just the same way she cares for the plant's machines—providing for them, making sure they can function smoothly, using them to their utmost capacity, delighting in the beauty of their efficiency and productivity. Is this love?

According to the description of love I have been using, these examples can both count as love. Yet instinctively we know that something is wrong with them. They may fit our description of love, but somehow they do not fit the criteria for the *kind* of love we expect when love is for human persons. They are in some way "false" loves, we think, or at least mistaken loves. Why? What is the standard, the norm, by which we can judge a love to be "true," to be good, or just, or even wise?[1]

We may think there is something wrong with a parental love that responds to a child *only* as a projection of the parent because our understanding of "parental" love includes an element of other-centered love. Or we may think that totally self-centered love does not accord with the model for loving taught by Jesus Christ. Both of these ways of thinking, however, hold in their explicit content something more. The fundamental reason there is something wrong with a parent's love that responds to a child merely as a projection of the parent is that the child is more than that. As a human person, the child is unique, destined to be in an important sense autonomous, able to take responsibility for his own life some day, able to come into union with others by knowledge and love. A love that fails to affirm the child's dignity as a person worthy of respect and love in and for himself (and not just as a means to his parents' fulfillment) is a false love. That is, it "misses the reality," or an important part of the reality, of the beloved. Hence, the actions that flow from such a love are likely to be destructive in some way.

Similarly, the reason we find something not right about an employer's love for workers that affirms them as if they were machines is that the workers *are not* machines. They are persons. An affective affirmation, a love, that is at variance with a significant part of their reality will be erroneous, or at least inadequate; and it can be so in a way that will end up negating rather than affirming their being as a whole. If it is love for the workers at all, it must be affirming *some* aspect of them, even though it is an aspect that is instrumental to the employer's ends. Insofar as it affirms this and only this, it is love, but it is a mistaken love; and if it is not merely mistaken but knowingly distorts the reality of the workers, then we may call it an unjust love.

What begins to emerge from considerations such as these is that the norm for a right love is the concrete reality of the beloved, of whoever or whatever is loved. Just as in regard to knowledge we identify the possibilities of ignorance and mistakes and lies, so in regard to love we can simply fail to love at all (the object in question), or we can love with a mistaken love (affirming some aspect of the beloved's reality in a way that unintentionally distorts the whole or misses an important part of it), and we can love with a "lying" love (intentionally ignoring and distorting aspects of the reality of the one loved). A love is right and good insofar as it aims to affirm truthfully the concrete reality of the beloved. This is what I mean by a "just love."

I use the term "just" love because of its traditional reference to something being "due." I intend to include in it something being due in the strict sense of a right and in a broader sense of what is "fitting." The concrete reality of what is loved constitutes the standard of what is "due," the norm according to which the justice, the truth, of our love must be measured.

To translate the notion of a just love into our overall considerations of commitment and obligation, however, some further observations are necessary. If, for example, the norm of a just love is the concrete reality of the beloved, everything will depend on how we interpret this reality. It is important to note that our knowledge of human persons generally, as well as of individual persons, obviously differs and changes, for our interpretation of human experience is both historical and social. To say this, I think, does not contradict the requirement of attending to concrete reality. Our very experience of the potential destructiveness as well as creativity of love prevents us from thinking that we can mold the reality of those we love solely according to our own wishes and subjective ideas. It gives us glimpses, too, of a reality in those we love that may cry out against the limits of our historically conditioned understandings.[2]

In general, it seems to me that we can say something like this of the concrete reality of human persons: Each is constituted with a complex structure—embodied, with a capacity for free choice, the ability to think and to feel, and so on.[3] Human persons are also essentially relational with interpersonal and social capacities and needs. They exist in the world, so that their reality includes their particular history and their involvement in social, political, economic, and cultural contexts. It includes their identification with, yet not complete limitation to, systems and institutions. Moreover, it includes not only their present actuality but the potentiality that each has for development, for human and individual flourishing—as well as the vulnerability each has for diminishment. Finally, human persons are unique as well as common sharers in humanity.

A just love of persons will, for example, affirm their essential equality as human persons, but it will also attend to the differences among them in terms of capabilities and needs. It will take account of and respect the essential autonomy of persons and the meaning and value that they themselves give to their lives (though it will not thereby abdicate its own responsibility for discerning meaning and values in the concrete lives of the ones loved). It will also take account of and respect the relationships that are as essential to persons as is their freedom or autonomy. With these and similar considerations we could develop here the basic ethical norms for a just love of persons. I think it is sufficient in the context of this chapter, however, simply to point in the direction of a more complete theory. Short of this full theory, we can nonetheless maintain that love will be just, in the sense of "accurate," when it does not destroy or falsify the reality of the person loved (either as human or as unique individual). It will be *more* or *less* just, in the sense of "adequate," as it more or less adequately reaches to the full and complex reality of the one loved. In this second sense justice in love admits of degrees.

In addition to these overall observations about the concrete reality of human persons, and the development of ethical principles to guide a just love of persons, other observations are important if we are to translate the idea of a just love into the context of commitment. The first of these goes like this: When I love another person, I place my own self in affirmation of the other.[4] Because of this, there is no love for another that does not entail some affirmation (whether true or false, adequate or inadequate) of myself. Even if the love is what we would call wholly "other-centered" love, it is my very self-affirmation that is placed in affirmation of the other. Hence, if love of another person is to be just, it must of necessity also be just in terms of its affirmation of myself. If as a way of loving it falsifies or distorts my concrete reality, it cannot be a just way of loving another. This is especially evident in the context of a committed love. If in making a commitment to love I am giving my word, placing my very self in some way in the keeping of the beloved (as an expression of and a seal on my love), I will do this justly only if I do it in a way that does not violate the concrete reality either of myself or of the one I love. For example, I may promise to love you in a way that fails to take account of my reality as already committed, or that aims to destroy myself by undermining in me any sense of autonomy; but if I do so, I do so unjustly. This touches on one of the most difficult aspects of commitment and obligation, and I will return to it shortly.

But one last observation about the general notion of justice in love and its relevance to discernment of commitment-obligation: The concrete reality of persons includes their relationships (as we have seen) and hence their commitments. For this reason, a just love cannot abstract from, but must attend to, these commitments. More specifically, if I have given a commitment to someone, I cannot now love that person justly unless I take account of the claim that she or he has on me (a claim that is part of the meaning of the concrete relationship between us, and hence part of the reality of each of us). My obligation to keep the commitment will cease only if and when the reality of the relationship has somehow changed—that is, if the reality of the relationship has changed so that the claim no longer is legitimately placed on me.

This brings us back to our central questions with a slightly new formulation: What sorts of changes in the reality of a committed relationship count as justifying reasons for breaking the commitment? as reasons that remove or override the claim that is at the heart of the commitment? Or when can our love be a just love despite our nonfulfillment of a specific commitment-obligation?

A JUST LOVE, RELEASED FROM ITS PROMISE

I have already said that, in my view, not all commitment-obligations "hold." It is possible for things to change within or surrounding a commitment-relationship so that the claim intrinsic to the commitment is released. There are three situations, I believe, in which this can be the case: (1) when it truly becomes impossible to sustain the commitment-relationship; (2) when a specific commitment-obligation no longer fulfills the purposes of the larger commitment it was meant to serve; and (3) when another obligation comes into conflict with, and supersedes, the commitment-obligation in question.

The three situations I am now proposing for consideration need not be viewed as mutually exclusive. Sometimes they offer different ways of seeing the same thing (as, for example, when destructive consequences can be interpreted as signaling the loss of the meaning of the commitment, or the impossibility of keeping it, or the presence of a conflicting and more serious obligation). I want, therefore, to try to clarify my understanding of these situations, their various conditions and their alternate emphases, less with a view to keeping the concepts clear and distinct from one another than with a concern to show in one way or another the sorts of changes in commitment-relations that produce reasons to justify the release of commitment-obligations.

To focus on just these three situations seems to leave out two of the traditional categories I identified in the previous chapter— the categories of "original meaning" and "release by the promisee." I do not want to deny the importance of these. Both of them will to some extent be incorporated into the descriptions of my present three categories (or what I am here calling "situations"). Moreover, it is important to note that sometimes conditions for release from obligation are an explicit part of the original content of the commitment ("built into the contract")—conditions such as mutual release by the parties of the commitment or grounds on which the commitment-obligation will be considered forfeit. It is not this kind of release from obligation that particularly concerns me here, for it does not (at least in principle) raise serious problems. Indeed, "release" from obligation in such cases could just as well be called "fulfillment" of obligation—for one reaches the limit of what one explicitly intended to yield to the other's claim. The situations I will describe here are situations where we have *not* fulfilled our obligations, but we are nonetheless released.

Impossibility

When it truly becomes impossible to sustain a commitment-relationship, it may belong to a just love to change or break the commitment. Impossibility of fulfillment has long been accepted as a justifying reason for release from the obligation of a promise. As we saw in chapter 6, there is something about this condition that leads us quite readily to accept its excusing function. After all, if I truly *cannot* fulfill what I have promised, it seems unfair and illogical to hold me accountable (unless perhaps my very incapacity is somehow my own fault).[5] However easily this conclusion seems to follow, the whole notion of "impossibility" bears further reflection.

Kinds of Impossibility

First of all, we need to distinguish different kinds of impossibility as they are relevant to release from commitments. There is, first, what can be described as "physical" impossibility. If I have promised to help friends move into a new home on a certain date and I am suddenly taken to the hospital with acute appendicitis, it is physically (and absolutely) impossible for me to fulfill my promise. No one in such a case will reasonably reproach me for my failure to keep my commitment. What R. M. Hare calls the "practical question" (of *whether* or not I will or can do something) simply does not arise.[6]

But there are other kinds of impossibility that may also release us from obligations to keep commitments. We are seldom at ease in determining these, however, and are often confused about what is required of us in the face of them. Part of the problem is that we do tend to think of ourselves as responsible for some forms of limitation in ourselves and in our relationships. This is true even when what we experience is true powerlessness. Another part of the problem is that impossibility, when it is not "physical," is less like an objective, incontrovertible "fact" and more like a judgment that we make or even a decision. The "practical question" can often still be raised, which means that it must be faced.

This "nonphysical" (sometimes called "psychological," sometimes "moral"[7]) impossibility is the kind that could exist for Stephen and Ann. The deterioration of their marriage relationship may be so serious that reconciliation has become, indeed, impossible. If so, no amount of effort to bridge the distance between them will be successful. What was once love is now so mixed with bitterness and hate that they simply cannot remain together without the utter destruction of themselves and the loss of even what Theodore Mackin calls "the most detached and cold wishing the best" for one another.[8]

Impossibility in this sense may also characterize Henry's situation. Perhaps the apathy and despair that cast a pall over his life and spirit are so complete that without a drastic change he will slowly, as a person, die. Unless a new future can open for him, he will cease psychologically (so to speak) to breathe.

Maybe even Helen, in her love for her new friend, Abe, has reached a point where it is impossible to "turn back" and restore relations with her husband. Whatever she might have done (and ought to have done) in the beginning of this new love, it may be too late now to let it go or to maintain it within the limits she had originally envisioned.

Perhaps Carey, after twenty-five years in her religious community, faces the fact that her struggles with persons in authority have left her turned in upon herself with an exaggerated scrupulosity and unable, in this context, to carry on fruitful ministry. This realization, along with the growing "thinkableness" of leaving the community and beginning a new life on her own, may make it literally impossible for her to stay.

In all these cases, it is clear just how difficult it is to make a judgment about "impossibility." Why, for example, cannot Ann and Stephen use all their courage and intelligence, with some wise help from others, to find the way of fidelity to one another? How can it be that their married love, once strong and peaceful, is now no longer possible to sustain? And Henry, "unhitched" as he is from the most important commitments in his life (his wife and children and occupation)—can he not call on memory and hope, can he not be brave in a night of the spirit, can he not trust that life is within him and around him and that he will experience it once again? Helen, too, may have reached a point of "no return" in her new love and her old, so that she can no longer balance them both, be faithful to both of them. But can she not do what others have done throughout human history? Can she not accept the tragic aspects of her life and heroically let go the love that conflicts with her primary and lifelong commitment to her husband and family? And why cannot Carey, especially now that she recognizes her lack of liberty of spirit and the possibility of changing authority structures, work to gain freedom *within* her community? Why does she have to leave it in order to do the work she feels called to do?

Determining Impossibility

No one must make the notion of "impossibility" a kind of "cheap grace" that easily removes our profound commitment-obligations. What is possible and what is not possible in all these situations cannot be determined apart from the concrete experience of those who live them. There are obvious critical questions to be asked about the accuracy of the analysis of any given situation and about the integrity in the personal motivation of those who are discerning and deciding. Nonetheless, "impossibility" as a legitimate reason for release from commitment-obligations remains.

In the abstract we can point to general ways in which we experience the psychological or moral impossibility of keeping our commitments. Sometimes, for example, the reality of the relationship to which we have committed ourselves seems simply gone. It no longer exists, and nothing that we do can retrieve it. The reality and any potentiality for a particular growing friendship, or a specific married love, or a partnership in a common enterprise may have ceased to exist. Our promise to sustain them has now no object, or its object is a juridical relationship that is essentially different from our intention when we promised.

Sometimes the relationship to which we have committed ourselves still exists, but it has become truly intolerable. What we somewhat antiseptically call *incompatibility*, for example, can gradually erode our tolerance for a shared life with particular persons, whether in marriage or any other form of relationship. More than this, there can be within a relationship *a conflict* so great that we can no longer endure it. Growing intractable and all-consuming irritation; moods endlessly whirling us away from each other; radical and comprehensive misunderstandings of deepest intentions; disagreement regarding the fundamental requirements of our commitment and its way of fidelity; vicious, active attacks mutually launched or with one the aggressor and the other the victim—at some point these aspects of our experience resist all "conflict resolution" and render our continuation in the relationship impossible.

If we ask how we know with certainty that we have reached the point at which fulfillment of our promise is impossible, no one answer can be given. It is clear, however, that a "threshold of impossibility" does indeed exist. It is in a different place in every individual relationship. No doubt in family relations it is in a different place from where it is in larger societal ones. (It is one thing, for example, to live with bitterness and resentment against an institution or its officers and remain a faithful politician or even a faithful church member; it is another thing to live with bitterness and resentment in the everyday relations of a household.) The "threshold of impossibility" may even be in a different place in kinship relations than it is in relations between persons who have loved with an intimate and freely chosen love. However different the place at which we encounter impossibility and however difficult it is to decide that we have come upon it, there is at least a potential point beyond which we are unable to go, or at least unable to go without terrible destruction to ourselves and to others.

Contributing Factors

Can we say anything about the factors that bring us to, or keep us from the threshold of impossibility? Why is one person able, for example, and another not able to keep commitments that are in some generic sense the same? One factor, obviously, is an individual's own moral strength, his inner resources for faithfulness, for survival in otherwise debilitating circumstances, for integrity and anchoring in courageous love. Not everyone is capable of either heroic perseverance or an imaginative sense of humor—whatever it takes to remain whole in the face of a greatly burdened commitment.

Of course, we all have limitations in our capacities to keep love alive and to resist conflicting loves. Some of these incapacities have always been beyond our individual power to overcome. We are not, then, responsible for them in the ordinary sense (though we may truthfully mourn them and even authentically repent of them, as when we repent at ever new awarenesses of our racism and sexism or when we experience true remorse for our specific moral weaknesses). These limitations and incapacities may derive from basic problems in temperament traceable to who knows what sources in our physiology, our innate intellectual powers, our cultural and economic limitations and deprivations, and so on. They may be the residue in us, or the essential signs, of our participation in the "human condition"—the condition of natural limitation and process (part of our glory as well as our misery) or the condition of shared sinfulness. They may also come from the past choices we have made, so that we are indeed responsible for them, even though we are now, in a particular situation, powerless to change them.

It would be a mistake, however, to think that the possibility of keeping commitments is only a matter of managing our own feelings or expanding the limits of our own powers of courageous love. In relationships that are meant to be mutual, that essentially involve interaction between myself and another person, what the other does or can do and what happens between us may make all the difference. We saw this positively, in terms of fidelity, in chapter 6. It holds here negatively as well, in terms of the grounds for release from obligation by reason of an authentic inability to keep it.

The other persons with whom I share commitments may make it impossible for me to fulfill my promises because of their own incapacities to sustain the relationship. They may also simply betray me, with ill will violate their own obligation in ways that make it impossible for the relationship to continue. In some societies and traditions, for example, certain actions have been thought to constitute grounds for divorce not just because the one who committed them thereby forfeited the right to faithfulness on the part of a partner (though that, too), but because the actions were so disruptive of the relationship that it could not afterward be restored. Such actions included adultery, nonsupport (on the part of a husband), abandonment or desertion, refusal to fulfill the "marriage debt" over a long period of time, and attempted murder of one's spouse. Similarly, heresy, rebellion, or violation of major disciplinary rules have constituted grounds on which churches have felt justified in eliminating communal obligations to members (hence "excommunicating" them). Whether or not we approve of the content of these examples, they serve to illustrate the role of the promisee in making our own fidelity possible.

Possibility or impossibility in promise-keeping may also be traced to factors other than the capabilities and actions of the individuals involved. Institutional structures and frameworks for commitment and the general milieu in which they are lived out are extremely important in this regard. As the sociologist Jessie Bernard observed, "The nature of the household in which a marriage functions is a powerful determinant of the nature of the relationship itself."[9]

For example, the ultimate source of the eventually tragic tension in the marriage between Kristin Lavransdatter and Erlend was probably not temperamental differences between the two of them.

It was the fact that they, with their differences, were bound in a marriage whose culturally established patterns of power could not hold those differences. The subtlety of this flashes for us momentarily when Erlend objects, with anguish as well as anger, to Kristin's bitter reminder of his past failures: "Much have I borne from you, Kristin, but I will no longer bear never to be left in peace for these old mischances, *nor to have you speak to me as though I were your thrall—*." Kristin, "shaking with passion," answers her husband:

> Never have I spoken to you as though you were a thrall. Have you *once* heard me speak harshly or angrily to any human being that could be *counted as lesser than I. . . .* But you should be my *master . . .* according to God's law, Erlend. And if so be I have lost patience, and have spoken to you in such wise as it befits not a wife to speak to her husband—I trow it has been because you have many a time made it hard for me to bow my simplicity before your better understanding, to honour and obey my husband and lord so much as I fain would have done—and maybe I looked that you—maybe I deemed I might spur you on to show that you were a man, and I but a poor simple woman.[10]

Cultural patterns, the entrenchment or transition of structural models, dissonance or harmony between individual expectations and social possibilities, economic pressures and deprivations, general societal order and the strength or weakness of religious symbols, institutional and personal "support systems"—all of these have tremendous impact on what can be achieved and sustained by persons in commitment-relationships.

Prevention and Restoration

A final way to try to understand the many factors involved in determining possibility and impossibility in given situations is to ask what might make possible the fulfillment of a commitment that would otherwise be impossible. I am not thinking of things like a sudden new strength of character, or a miraculous cessation of conflict, or a radical change in the whole context of the commitment. I am, however, thinking about three sorts of changes in the commitment-relationship, changes that might prevent or reverse an approach to the threshold of impossibility.

The first of these is the most obvious. That is, if what makes it impossible to go on in a commitment-relationship is the particular framework that structures the relationship, then restructuring—even radical restructuring—may restore possibility. "Framework" has many levels of meaning, of course. There is the level at which, for example, "marriage" and "religious congregation" and "friendship," are frameworks that structure our relationships into generic forms. There is also the level where framework means a certain cultural model of any of these kinds of generic relationships (as when, for example, marriage is based on a patriarchal model or on a model of partnership between equals). And finally there is the level of framework that is the particular structure worked out by the particular participants in any relationship. Change in structure at any of these levels may push back the threshold of impossibility. I shall say more about the most radical, generic level of structure later—for in a sense it offers a special case; that is, change in it may seem to constitute not a continuation but a break in the commitment-relation. At any rate, as soon as we begin to consider the practical change necessary in the framework of a commitment, we can sometimes see new hope for faithfulness. At other times, of course, we see just how impossible the fulfillment of some commitment-obligations is, for we see also how impossible some of its remedies are.

A second kind of change that may prevent or reverse impossibility has to do with our way of *thinking about a* commitment-relationship and its obligation. Obviously we cannot, just by thinking, change every impossible situation into one that is possible. Even if we could do this, we ought not to, for sometimes this would entail covering over what is in fact utterly destructive. On the other hand, it is true that our *interpretation* of a situation can contribute to its being closed or open to possibility for us.

One illustration of this is to be found in what Bernard calls the "revolution of rising expectations" regarding marriage.[11] Because marriage is thought to be able to provide a certain kind of happiness, a context for a just love, individual and shared growth, and so on, it becomes intolerable when a given marriage falls too far short of this expectation. "We do not tolerate today forms of marital behavior that were matter-of-fact in the past."[12] On the other hand, if marriage is thought of ultimately as a "juridical category *in which* they [the spouses] exist . . . not different from the existence, say, of a person's citizenship,"[13] it may hold certain hopes but not expectations that become requirements for its possibility (or, as we shall see shortly, for its meaning). Closely related to this, the perceived feasibility of more easily dissolving a marriage, and the existence of alternative "thinkable" options, probably lowers the threshold of impossibility. "Options make great demands. One of the oldest arguments against divorce is that, if people knew they had no choice, no way out, they would learn to live with one another, reconciled if not satisfied. Introduce the possibility of divorce and they become miserable."[14]

My point here is not to commend one or another way of thinking about marriage. It is only to show that our way of thinking about our commitments influences profoundly the possibility or impossibility of our fulfilling them. This means that even when our expectations are high regarding a commitment-relation, the *nature* of our expectations and their anchor as well as their flexibility will determine to an important extent the level of the threshold of impossibility. For example, if marriage (or lifelong intimate partnership) is believed to have tenderness as its major emotional goal and not passion, the possibility of lifelong faithfulness may be greater. Or if we understand that complete mutuality is not to be expected in any relationship, it may actually be more possible for us to fulfill our promises of mutual love. Or if we think about the church in the manner of Dorothy Day, some forms of impossibility may remain at the margins of our commitment:

> I loved the Church for Christ made visible. Not for itself, because it was so often a scandal to me. Romano Guardini said that the Church is the Cross on which Christ was crucified; one could not separate Christ from His Cross, and one must live in

a state of permanent dissatisfaction with the Church. . . . I felt
that the Church was the Church of the poor . . . that it cared for
the emigrant, it established hospitals, orphanages, day nurseries,
houses of the Good Shepherd, homes for the aged, but at the
same time I felt that it did not set its face against a social order
which made so much charity in the present sense of the word
necessary. I felt that charity was a word to choke over. . . .[15]

Because, as we shall see, the reasons for not keeping some
commitments go beyond the question of possibility and impossibility,
the goal in our efforts to interpret, to think about, our commitments
is not merely to make them possible. It is to approach more and
more closely to the truth of the situation, and to make possible an
ever increasing just love.

One last sort of change in a commitment-relationship that may
make it after all sustainable is the introduction of forgiveness—by
one or by both parties in the commitment. Without its offer in some
form at critical junctures in the process of living out a commitment,
probably no commitment-obligation remains possible of fulfillment
in the long run. The trouble with recommending forgiveness is,
however, that its own possibility depends (like the possibility of
fidelity generally) on the capacities of the persons involved and
on the corrigibility or ultimate bearableness of the problems in
the relationship. Still, there is a way in which forgiveness provides
an option different from simply holding strong and different from
ignoring or avoiding the harm that has ensued in relationship. It is
different, too, from despair in the face of offense, surrender to the
impossibility of transforming betrayal in a relationship that holds.
At its best it is active, not passive, and it serves to mobilize the
human spirit. It is the opposite both of hardening one's heart and
of allowing oneself to be victimized. Though it requires an inner
surrender, it is ultimately an expression of inner power. It can make
repentance possible as well as respond to repentance's plea. In so
doing, sometimes forgiveness succeeds in keeping a mutual life and
love from the threshold of certain kinds of impossibility.

At this point, however, new importance appears for the whole
"way of fidelity" that we explored in chapters 4 and 5. When our

question is one of the prevention of impossibility and the fulfillment of our commitments, the answers lie mainly in the traversing of this way. The obligation to keep our commitments extends to our efforts to keep them possible of fulfillment. My original assertion stands, however: When it is truly impossible to sustain a commitment-relationship, a just love may change or break it. But let me turn now to the second situation in which I have said a commitment-obligation may not hold.

Loss of Meaning

When a specific commitment no longer fulfills the purposes of the larger and more basic commitment that it was meant to serve, it may be a part of a just love to change it or break it. What I am concerned with here is the kind of situation in which a commitment seems to have lost its point. There may still be a relationship; it may be possible to sustain it in some way but it has lost its meaning. It is not just that I no longer seem to "experience" its meaning, to feel engaged in what I see still to be meaningful. The meaning is, as far as I can discern, gone. This can happen in two ways: (1) I may judge that I was completely mistaken about the worthwhileness of the ultimate object of a commitment; or (2) I may find that an instrumental commitment, intended to mediate, implement, or fulfill another more ultimate commitment, has lost its connectedness with what is more ultimate. In either case, the commitment seems to have lost its point. Here I want to focus primarily on the second case, the case of instrumental commitments. Though it looks like the simpler of the two, it can be, in fact, the more problematic. This is because it is not always clear what is instrumental and what is ultimate, or absolute, in our commitments.

Commitments as Instrumental

Let me begin with an example. Susan may consider ending her commitment to work in a given social service agency because in her judgment the agency no longer fulfills its stated goals of providing shelter for the homeless. Susan's most basic commitment is to work with and for homeless persons. Her colleagueship with the other founding members of this particular agency is terribly important to them and to her. Their history together has been one of great growth for all of them, and together they have been able to achieve truly marvelous results for the homeless in their city. Yet Susan has come to the conclusion that the work of the agency is no longer needed—not because there are no more housing needs such as the agency addressed in the past, but because the agency's structure (as she perceives it) does not allow it to adapt to changing political and economic situations that are extremely important if the work of sheltering is to go forward. Despite the fact that Susan had committed herself for another three years to the agency, she feels justified in breaking that commitment. It has in her view lost its meaning in relation to her larger commitment.

We could ask, of course, if Susan's analysis of the situation is accurate. After all, it is easy to look with a "suspicious stare" at any institution, see only its limitations, and fail to appreciate the greater life and continuing possibilities within it. We might want to ask, too, whether Susan's recent struggles with her more ultimate commitment to ministry have not lowered her tolerance for the ordinary frustrations in every concrete enterprise—so that her question of commitment-obligation is misplaced. That is, her real difficulty may be not with the agency but with her overall commitment to sheltering the homeless. Along with this question might go the question of whether she will continue in this ministry once she breaks her connection with the persons who have shared her commitment. Despite these questions, most of us can see the possible wisdom in Susan's judgments and the justice in her decision to move out of the agency. All other things being equal, we might applaud her decision as one of fidelity not betrayal, one of courage not weakness or hypocrisy.

Of course, not all other things are equal—precisely because Susan has made a promise to some particular persons. Suppose that her co-workers not only want her to remain with the agency through the time of her commitment, but they *need* her to remain. Suppose her participation is essential for the agency to continue at all. The whole point of the commitment made mutually by all of them was their need to be able to count on one another—to count on one another *even if* one of them should decide that the enterprise was not worthwhile. Do these co-workers not continue to have a claim on Susan?

On the above suppositions, the others in the agency do continue to have a claim on Susan. Yet it may not be an overriding claim. She must weigh the importance of the claim to them on the one hand, and on the other hand the importance of the fundamental commitment that gave meaning to this claim (for her) in the first place. In the balance, the fact that her commitment to this agency has not only lost its meaning but now contradicts this meaning may lead her to conclude that she is no longer bound to fulfill her promise to her co-workers. She could, it seems to me, be justified in drawing this conclusion.

Commitments Instrumental to Love

Is this same sort of analysis possible in principle when persons contemplate being dispensed from vows to a religious community and when persons consider divorce from their marriage partners? Because we tend to think of these commitments as less clearly instrumental than Susan's (that is, hers to the agency), as more likely to be ends in themselves, their mediation of other commitments seems more difficult to take seriously.

Yet there is a profound sense in which religious vows in community and marriage vows are not themselves ultimate, absolute, unconditional commitments. For example, the point of traditional Christian vows of poverty, celibacy, and obedience is the constitution of a way of life conducive to growth in and expression of love for God and human persons, a way of life that includes building a community of life and worship and that is somehow ordered to corporate and individual ministry. Now if the experience of an individual in a given community is such that (at least for her) in this context growth in love (*agape*) is impossible, or ministry is an irremediably false witness to this love, or the essentials of communal life are hopelessly distorted, can it not be the case that this person is no longer obligated by her vows in and to this community? The claim originally yielded to the community has lost its point. The obligation that does exist is to the love that was the original reason for the vows—an obligation, therefore, to find another way to love justly, perhaps another framework in which to incarnate the expression and the strivings of the original love.

The case may seem more difficult with marriage vows. It is true here, too, that commitment (to a married love) can be understood relative to a fundamental love for God and for all human persons. Yet it also obviously involves profound obligations to specific persons, obligations that must not be trivialized by appeals made to a commitment beyond them. But the point, the meaning (derivative from the purpose), of marriage vows is historically complex. It is understood as stabilizing and expressing a relationship that can include a variety of meanings and purposes: the love between spouses, procreation and nurture of children, maintenance of family continuity and kinship systems, social identity and prestige, allocation of property, social control, economic security, sacramental witness to religious realities, the formation of a center of life conducive to an expanding love and service of God and neighbor, and so forth.

To talk of a cultural "institutional" meaning of marriage may seem to miss the fact that particular spouses can have quite different, even countercultural meanings for their marriage. I do not intend to exclude such meanings. What I do exclude, though, are purely personal motivations that individuals have—personal and private motivations that do not constitute some common meaning for both spouses and for the wider community (after all, even countercultural meanings are somehow understandable in terms of what they aim to transform). Personal reasons for marriage (which can range from love for one's spouse to a need for security to a desire for status or companionship or children or emotional support or a way to escape from one's family of origin) can coincide with a common understanding of marriage or not. Insofar as they do not, the fact that a marriage does not satisfy them does not necessarily mean that the marriage obligation does not hold. In other words, what I am talking about here is not the nonfulfillment of a uniquely personal purpose for marriage (though that might bear some consideration in its own right) but the meaning (and possible loss of meaning) of "marriage" as it is experienced in a given commitment to married love.

Suppose that in a particular society marriage has only one meaning, one purpose (and that in a particular marriage the spouses subscribe to this meaning or some variant of it). Then if one or both of the spouses determine that their own specific marriage has failed of this meaning, that it contradicts this purpose, will it not follow that the obligation to sustain the marriage can be released? That the point of the marriage is gone?

For example, suppose marriage is understood solely as a way of procreating and rearing children. If a given marriage is unable to mediate this purpose, the obligation of the spouses may be removed. Or suppose marriage is understood as essentially a way to assure the future of a mutually shared love (and a life of committed love of God and neighbor). If the marriage framework (either marriage as such, or marriage on a particular structural model, or the entrenched pattern of this particular marriage) comes to militate against this love, can the marriage and its obligations have any point? Or if the ultimate point of marriage is thought to be to provide a witness to the graced life of the church, will not any marriage that falsifies that witness (and that cannot be made true) lose the force of obligation that would otherwise have been at its center?

Now of course no society or religious tradition understands marriage to have only one purpose. Not even contemporary Western society affirms only one reason for marriage (for while love and companionship between spouses may have become the primary reason acknowledged in our society, this does not exclude an essential concern for the bearing and rearing of children or for the role of the family as a part of a whole society). But my point in separating out the various meanings of marriage is to allow us to see that marriage, too, is relative to the purposes it serves. Having seen this, some observations follow.

First, perhaps in practice the obligation entailed by marriage vows can never be released in the way I am suggesting. For if there is always more than one *raison d'être* for marriage, every marriage will probably fulfill at least one of the purposes. Even if the personal love that partners originally had for one another wanes, for example, their marriage still has meaning as a matrix for rearing children. Even if that fails, it has meaning insofar as it contributes to social order (that is, as long as it abides, it at least does not constitute a destabilizing example for other marriages). And so on.

Yet, in fact, it is possible to think of marriages whose tragedy is that they are unable to serve any of the reasons for marriage. If this stretches the imagination, it is not difficult to think of marriages where the inability to realize one of the reasons for marriage is so serious that it overshadows the importance of the others and leads to the conclusion that, overall, this marriage no longer has a meaning that can make its obligation hold.

Suppose Sheila, for example, becomes certain that Joshua has never really loved her, never even in a general sense affirmed her well-being. Suppose he has even told her that he wants to continue the marriage solely because it suits his career ambitions and provides him with a home and caretaker for his children. In this situation, the last vestiges of Sheila's original love for Joshua are threatened. Moreover, the distance between them makes it difficult for her to respond to their children. While acknowledging the multiple obligations entailed by her marriage vows (including obligations to the wider community), Sheila may nonetheless conclude that to continue this marriage will contradict the original love she promised to Joshua and the love for her children that she promised in her original decision to bear them. Ironically, faithfulness to these commitments to love may require her to end a marriage (in which she would gradually negate her love) and to disband a household (in which she cannot nurture her children).

What do these illustrations show us overall about our obligation to keep commitments once they cease to fulfill the fundamental purposes they were meant to serve? They show most obviously, I suppose, the difficulties of discerning when the meaning of commitment has so changed that its obligation ceases. There are, as I have acknowledged repeatedly, the problems of accurate analysis of a given situation and honest evaluation of our own desires for change. There is always the risk of reducing the obligation of all of our commitments to the narrow measure of our own private purposes and our desires (and hence to confuse the very notion of obligation). But there is also the problem of seeming to relativize even the most important commitments in our lives, making means out of what we think of as ends, interpreting as instrumental what we usually consider fundamental. If we can judge even marriage and vows in religious communities and lifelong commitments to ministry, by reason of their mediation or lack of mediation of something more fundamental than themselves, what will finally count as ultimate in our commitments? At the very least we must say, I think, that central to what ultimately counts is the love we have chosen and choose and the objects of that love.

The Ultimate in the Commitment to Love

When a specific commitment no longer fulfills the purposes of the more basic commitment that it was meant to serve, it may belong to a just love to change it or break it. What emerges from our considerations thus far, ironically, is a more stringent view of the obligation of fidelity to the love we promised but at the same time, and in that very obligation, a reason for release from commitment-obligations of a very serious kind. Let me try to clarify this.

However surprising it may seem at this point in our explorations, we must affirm that there is something unconditional about the obligation entailed by our commitments to love persons. That is, unless there was something wrong or mistaken about the love we promised in the first place (when we first committed ourselves to it), there are at least two reasons why *we are not ever released from the obligation to love* the person or group to whom we gave our promise. How can I say this when I have already said several times (and am in the midst of trying to demonstrate) that our commitments do not always "hold"?

The first reason why we are not ever released from a commitment to love someone is that this commitment-obligation participates in our *fundamental obligation to love all persons* insofar as they are persons. I am here assuming this fundamental obligation, but it is implied in what I have maintained regarding the concrete reality of persons. Each person, and every person, is worthy of love as an end in herself. Not only are persons worthy of love, they by their very existence call us, obligate us, to love them—to affirm affectively their well-being, to refrain from harming them unjustly and to do positive good for them within the limits of what is ethically required. However illusory may have been our perceptions of a person in regard to her particular characteristics, she remains as a person fundamentally lovable. When we promise to love someone or a group of persons, we promise what is in a real sense already obligated just because we share humanity. In this general sense, our promise to love is unconditional.

But, of course, we promise more than this. By reason of our promise, we give the one we love a special claim on us, a claim that will in some way (according to the terms of the commitment) give him or her a *special right* to call us to love and to the deeds of love. In our promise of a special love lies the second reason why we are obligated to continue to love (as best we can), as well as the reason why we can be released from specific promises. The key to this paradox lies in the fact that our commitments to love are almost always commitments to love in certain ways, commitments to certain frameworks for living out our love. If we hope to use this paradoxical key, we must turn again to the connections among our love and our desire to make commitments to love and our tendency to form those commitments into certain frameworks for living our love.

Why do we tie our commitments to love with commitments to certain frameworks for love (frameworks like marriage, religious community, special causes and projects)? The answer to this question lies in our reasons for making commitments at all. But why *do* we make commitments, especially commitments to love—to love God or human persons? What is the "point" of them? As we saw in chapter 3, we commit ourselves to love at least partly because we want to stabilize our loves in the midst of the fickleness of our feelings. We want to give our loves a future by embodying them in a framework that makes ongoing demands upon us, that keeps us together with one another and attentive and awake, that allows us to share our lives and to grow as we collaborate in mutual concern and mutual enterprise. We want to form and to express our loves as "special" loves, as more whole, more unconditional, more intimate, more trustworthy than all the other loves we try to give. We want sometimes to give our lives to making the world a home where those we love—particular persons and, universally, all persons—can survive and flourish, in union one with another. These are some of the reasons why our commitments tend to take the form of commitment to a framework for love and for living—the framework of marriage, a certain life-style, concrete forms of action, community structures, patterns of friendship, and so on. Our hope is that in and by these frameworks our love will endure and flourish, and we shall learn the evolving demands and deeds of love and yield its fruits.

But if it does not prove so—if within and even because of a given framework our love is weakened or we threaten to destroy one another, if this framework turns out to obscure what we love or we find ourselves tragically ill-suited to what may serve the lives of others well, or even if this framework mediates our love but another framework can mediate *this same love* better, then the obligation to our particular form of commitment may not hold. It may be the better part of a just love to change it.

The requirement here is to discern what is essential to our basic commitment to love another and what is accidental to it. To acknowledge that frameworks take their meaning and value from the love they are meant to mediate is not to say that they are of minor significance or that they may easily be severed from the obligation of the basic commitment to love. Indeed, quite the opposite. But this point of view does entail the conclusion that all frameworks of love are conditional and all commitments to them are relative. Some aspects of them, relative to the basic commitment to love, may be essential for the basic commitment. If so (if this condition holds—as well as the positive conditions in the other two situations I am describing in this chapter), then these must never slip outside of the claim we have yielded in making our promise. But other aspects may prove their own inadequacy for mediating the love we have promised.

Should we be justified in changing the framework of a commitment, the special claim we have given to our love still obligates in some way. Even when we must end a marriage or leave a community or withdraw from a project, the special right of the other at least obligates us, to the extent we are able, to change the commitment with care, without violence on our part, with some form of fidelity to the love we originally promised. Given the tumultuous endings of some forms of relationship, the pain and possible oppression, it is difficult to speak of the obligation of love in ending, in leaving, in repudiating. We tread here close to hollow rhetoric, to a lack of realism and a compounding of the burden of loss or failure. Yet the commitment-obligation to a fundamental love does hold even through the changing of the instrumental commitment that was meant to serve it.

Within our promise, then, lies the basis for our being released from it and the basis for our continuing to be bound. A just love, committed unconditionally, may require that its framework be lived to the end; but it may also require that its framework be changed.

Let me turn now to the third situation out of which a reason justifying the breaking of commitments may emerge. In many respects it is like the situation I have just been trying to describe, and it pushes us to the same kinds of insights. What makes it different is that it addresses not the conflict between ultimate and proximate obligations within one commitment-relation but the conflict between a specific commitment-obligation and an obligation grounded in some other way.

Alternate Superseding Obligation

When another obligation comes into conflict with and supersedes the obligation to keep a commitment, a just love may require that the commitment be broken or changed. I have already described in chapter 6 the kind of situation in which we experience competing claims on our faithfulness. We have seen, then, something of the variety of ways in which this can happen. For example, conflict can arise because other moral principles besides the principle of promise-keeping apply in any given situation. (My obligation to keep my word can be in tension with my obligation to prevent serious harm to someone or with my obligation to tell the truth or to express gratitude, and so on.) In addition, there can be conflict specifically between two or more commitment-obligations (as when fulfilling a promise to a friend comes into conflict with keeping my commitments to my parents, or when loyalty to my country conflicts with faithfulness to an organization to which I belong).

One or many persons, others or my own self, can be the objects of these conflicting claims. Thus, the conflict may regard differing obligations to the same person (the one who has received my promise), as when I am torn between my pledge of confidentiality to my friend and my concern to prevent her from committing suicide. Or the conflict may be between one person and another, as when I must decide to keep a commitment to my family that conflicts with a commitment to my co-workers or when I find that fulfilling a promise to a political action group will bring harm to a whole city. Or, finally, the conflict may be between faithfulness to another person and responsibility to myself, as when continuance in a partnership requires the sacrifice of my own professional interests.

All of these kinds of conflict are important enough to warrant careful consideration. I am going to concentrate, however, only on potential conflicts between the duties we have (through one or more commitments) to more than one person, and on the conflicts that may occur between duties to ourselves and duties to those we have promised to love. What we can learn here of the nature of some conflicts may show that some commitment-obligations do not hold precisely because another obligation supersedes.

Conflicting Commitments to Others

I will not attempt anything like a complete analysis of the conflicts we can experience in our commitments to more than one person. Some observations about these conflicts can be helpful, however, if we are to understand the options that are ours within them. First of all, it seems to me essential to recognize that in many situations of competing obligations the conflict does not run so deep that the commitment-relation as a whole is in question. Oftentimes the conflict is not over who or what to love but over what actions can be performed in relation to different loves. So, for example, when Augustine chooses to "give the weak preference over the strong," to offer his time and energy to the vast numbers in his congregation rather than to his closest friends, he understands himself not as breaking his overall commitment to his friends but only as postponing "as a mark of trust" the deeds of friendship for a time. It is his perception that this conflict is not finally about whom to love but about which deeds of love ought to be done in this time and place. We might ask, of course, whether his friends shared his perception, and whether his judgment was accurate and just. But the point is that love is not to be equated with specific *deeds* of love when the latter are not possible or called for. The crucial matter for discernment in such situations, then, is what deeds are "called for"—in terms of urgency and seriousness of need, the nature of the commitment-relation, the implications for the common good, and whatever else constitutes ground here for a moral claim. When all deeds are not possible (at the same time or ever), which ones, in which relationships, take priority? The answer to this question is not necessarily correlative to which relationships are most important.

For example, suppose Harriet on a given afternoon is about to leave the social service agency where she works. She has promised her daughter to attend the rehearsal of a concert in which she will play. Just as Harriet is leaving, a client calls with desperation in her voice: There has been a fire in the client's home and she has nowhere to take her family. Harriet's decision to miss the rehearsal in order to arrange temporary housing for her client is not a decision either to break her overall commitment as a mother to her daughter or to love her client more than her daughter. Yet it is likely that she is not obligated to fulfill her specific promise to her daughter.

Of course, an example like this points up the inherent difficulties in what some call "love's casuistry." Harriet's obligation to keep her promise in this case may indeed not "hold." She, however, may experience not only regret but remorse (especially if this sort of situation has developed many times before, and she knows her daughter will not easily understand). And perhaps the removal of the commitment-obligation is not so easy as it seems, for this incident may be bound up with a whole series of conflicts that make Harriet unsure of the wisdom and fidelity of her actions. In any case, this example stands as one in which the whole of a commitment-relation is probably not at stake.

But we must go on to acknowledge that sometimes, indeed, a conflict between obligations is radical enough to place a commitment-relation as a whole in question. To say this is not necessarily to contradict what I have said earlier in this chapter about a fundamental obligation to love. That is, if a conflict of obligations should turn out to justify nonfulfillment of a major lifelong commitment, this does not thereby justify ceasing to love altogether the one to whom love has been promised. As we saw before, so it is true here, too: At the very least, the love that is owed to all persons as persons is still owed to this one, and the special love that has been promised may still require *some* actualization even if the original framework of obligation as such is released. Whatever the conflict, it is not to be resolved by refusing fundamental love.

Yet even if fundamental love is not to be repudiated, an overall *way* of loving (once again, the framework for the love) may indeed be in conflict with another value or another commitment. Dorothy Day, for example, wrote of her dread decision to leave her common-law husband when she determined to be baptized in the Roman Catholic church:

> We both suffered in body as well as in soul and mind. He would not talk about the faith and relapsed into complete silence if I tried to bring up the subject. The point of my bringing it up was that I could not become a Catholic and continue living with him, because he was averse to any ceremony before officials of either Church or State. He was an anarchist and an atheist, and he did not intend to be a liar or a hypocrite. He was a creature of utter sincerity, and however illogical and bad-tempered about it all, I loved him. It was killing me to think of leaving him. . . . By winter the tension had become so great that an explosion occurred and

we separated again. When he returned, as he always had, I would not let him in the house; my heart was breaking with my own determination to make an end, once and for all, to the torture we were undergoing.[16]

In such decisions, we are inclined to say that the whole relationship is let go. It may be true that love continues—both a general love (such as we are to have for all persons) and a special love (in the sense that the relationship continues to hold special meaning for us and have *some* special claim on us); but there is a critical sense in which it is also left behind. Something in the commitment-obligation is changed, broken, even though something may forever continue. And the decision is not made primarily on the basis of what this particular love demands in order not to be destroyed or in order to be implemented in the only way possible (though this cannot be completely ignored). It is made primarily on the basis of the demands, the call, of another love.

This is the kind of conflict between claims that the philosopher Stuart Hampshire is talking about when he describes a conflict between "two ways of life." His example is that of someone who "has a mission, to which he is dedicated, which cannot now be fulfilled without his leaving his family behind—a desertion that will make them unhappy. He either goes or he stays, and there is no middle way."[17] And, we must add, if he goes, he not only makes his family unhappy; he is probably breaking his commitment-obligation to them.

Such conflicts emerge only from deep within our experience, and they are inseparable from our central beliefs, our life histories, the choices we have heretofore made. Not everyone is confronted by this kind of choice, and sometimes those who are have mistaken a choice of both/and for one of either/or. Yet we all know the possibility of such conflict and the task of discernment it carries with it. What I am insisting on here is that it *can* be the case that a commitment-obligation—even one that is central in our lives— will be overridden by another obligation; and in this way there is justification for changing or breaking the commitment.

Obligation to Self and Commitment-Obligation to Another

Perhaps in twenty-first-century Western culture the obligation most often perceived to be in conflict with commitment-obligations is the obligation we have to ourselves. In many ways it is this conflict that offers the most disturbing questions for us. Can a concern for our own well-being (especially our own self-fulfillment) really weigh in the balance against the obligation to keep our promises (especially our profound promises to love another)? Can an obligation to ourselves really ever "count" as a justifying reason to change or break marriage vows, lifelong promises to God through commitment to a religious community, pledges of companionship and love in serious friendship, commitments to projects that demand lifelong labor and loyalty?

The answer of contemporary European and American culture seems to be a resounding "yes." The interchange between Nora and Helmer, her husband, in Henrik Ibsen's *A Doll's House* has been repeated in countless similar partings (by whatever analogous partners) and rehearsed in countless anxious imaginations:

> *Nora.* I want to leave right away. Kristine should put me up for the night—
> *Helmer.* You're insane! You've no right! I forbid you! . . . It's outrageous. So you'll run out like this on your most sacred vows.
> *Nora.* What do you think are my most sacred vows?
> *Helmer.* And I have to tell you that! Aren't they your duties to your husband and children?
> *Nora.* I have other duties equally sacred.
> *Helmer.* That isn't true. What duties are they?
> *Nora.* Duties to myself.
> *Helmer.* Before all else, you're a wife and mother.
> *Nora.* I don't believe in that anymore. I believe that, before all else, I'm a human being, no less than you—or anyway, I ought to try to become one.[18]

While we tend to take for granted that we have some responsibilities to ourselves, and some claims for self-love that set limits to our commitment-obligations, it is hardly ever completely clear how great must be our burden if it is to outweigh the duty we have undertaken by giving someone our word.

Overall patterns in our lives, as well as specific choices between particular competing claims, lead theologians and philosophers (and psychologists and social theorists) to worry about the need for "rules of preference" regarding ourselves and others.[19] Are we to love ourselves more than others or on a par with them? or are we to love others more than ourselves? Questions like these can be extremely complex, even when they are limited to efforts to understand the content of Christian *agape*. *Agape*, of course, has a normative meaning that in general repudiates loving ourselves more than others and that in a powerful sense calls for loving others more than ourselves. Yet debate continues over the place of self-love within or in relation to *agape*—over the meaning, for example, of equality in love as it applies to the lover as well as the loved, and over the meaning of self-sacrifice as it is translated into particular circumstances. I have no intention here of trying to resolve these issues. What I do want to do is to offer some ways of thinking about them when they appear at the heart of our most significant commitment-relations.

In fact, it is obvious that some self-sacrifice is morally required if we assume a commitment-obligation. There are several reasons why this is so. We live, for example, in a finite world where not every claim can be met and not every need fulfilled. It is not just the claims of others upon us that can conflict. Our own needs and the needs of those to whom we are committed also sometimes compete. But part of why we make a commitment is to clarify boundaries beyond which we will not assert our own claims. In addition, we ourselves are not whole and harmonious within ourselves so that the claim we yield to another may conflict with our own different desires. But, again, part of why we make the commitment is to assure the one to whom we give our word that we will not revoke it just because conflicting desires arise within us. We intend to ask of ourselves some sacrifice in relation to those desires; we intend to bind ourselves by duty to sacrifice what will negate our greater love.

More even than all of this, we can grow in our promised love to the point where we truly love the other (to whom we are committed) more than ourselves. We are willing, and we may experience ourselves called, to sacrifice everything we possess, even our lives, in order to do what is necessary for the well-being and happiness of the beloved.

And, finally, there is a way of coming into union with the one we love that requires our passing through the paradox of self-sacrifice— the paradox of losing one's self, yet finding it. The fullness of relation is approached only insofar as we let go of self-preoccupation. The reason for this lies in a basic interpretation of what it means to be a person. Central to our personhood is the capacity to come into union by knowledge and love with all reality and especially with other persons, other centers of consciousness and freedom. As persons we are ends in ourselves (hence not unworthy of "preoccupation") not only because we are free and self-determining but because we can know and be known, love and be loved in a way that expands, transcends, and completes our very selves. As we cease to exist only within and for ourselves (move beyond self-preoccupation), we come paradoxically to fuller possession of ourselves. We are centers of life, capable (without contradiction) of being centered more and more in ourselves as we are centered more and more beyond ourselves in others. But the way to this involves profound self-sacrifice. To love another with a just and faithful love turns out to mean that we affirm both the other's good and our own, though what we intentionally seek and ultimately choose may be only the good of the other. As it has often been said, ours is a reward that we find only when it is no longer what we primarily seek. Sometimes our commitments take us all the way to this.

From all of these reasons it follows that commitment involves, even requires, self-sacrifice. But it also follows that self-love and love of another are not necessarily incompatible. And that self-sacrifice is not necessarily incompatible with self-love. And, finally, that self-fulfillment not only need not be in opposition to the faithful love of another but may, in fact, be realized through it.

But if commitment obviously includes self-sacrifice, it is just as obvious that there are limits to the sacrifice that is required or even morally allowed. Self-sacrifice can destroy as well as contribute to true relationship. There are reasons for this as well. At the basis of them is the principle I earlier asserted: A just love requires a right love of oneself as well as of others. To place my self-affirmation in affective affirmation of another (which is what love of another is) requires that I do so in a way that takes account of the reality of us both. This means that, whatever fundamental demands there are for a right love of persons, these are also demands for the valuing of oneself. In other words, some *moral obligations* are grounded in one's own reality as a human person like other human persons. Ibsen's Nora was right: "Before all else, I'm a human being, no less than you—or anyway, I ought to try to become one."

This translates practically into a moral obligation not to relate to another person in a way that is truly destructive of ourselves as persons. It does not mean that we ought never to sacrifice our own welfare—sacrifice even our home, our health, our security, our reputation, our professional future, our very life. For who is to say that such sacrifice is never "fitting," never appropriate to a committed love, "if the cause be just"?

What it does mean (to say that we must not relate to others in ways destructive of ourselves as persons) is that while we may sacrifice everything we have, we may not sacrifice everything we are. We may not sacrifice in a final sense our autonomy. We may not sacrifice our capability for union and communion with God and human persons. The paradox here is that, should our love lead us to be willing to sacrifice even these essential aspects of ourselves (as great saints and lovers have sometimes desired in the extravagance of their love), we could not do so. For in so choosing, we would exercise our autonomy, and in yielding relation for the sake of a just love, we would make relation more possible. Without this kind of choice, however, and without a just love, it is possible to violate our obligation to ourselves and to destroy ourselves as persons.

It is insight into matters like these that led traditional Christian moral theologians to argue that we may give everything for love of another but we may not "sin" in so doing. We may not contradict our very selves or (in the terms I have been using) give a love that is *unjust* to another and consider what we do to be good. It is this same limit-setting insight that nonetheless opens the possibility of radical self-sacrifice. It is this traditional, and paradoxical, belief that Karl Rahner articulated thus:

It is an error and a heresy of modern eudemonism to believe that what is morally right can never lead one to a tragic destiny for which there is no solution in terms of this world. Christians must literally be prepared, as something almost to be expected, that their Christian commitment will inevitably lead them, one day or another, to a situation in which they must sacrifice everything rather than lose their own soul.[20]

Ah, but the criterion of *a just love* remains all important. For obligations to ourselves *can* prohibit certain forms of self-sacrifice, and they can, therefore, justify release from commitment-obligations. In some commitments, it is fairly clear that demands that exceed the reasonable limits of our promise do not obligate us. But even in relationships where it is "fitting" to go beyond the strict demands of minimal justice, there are limits beyond which we ought not to go. When demands are made on us (or we think they are made) that violate our very personhood or that are based on false needs in the other or that see sacrifice as an end in itself, it does not belong to a just love to fulfill them. When demands are made that burden us "beyond reason" or beyond our strength, it need not belong to a just love to fulfill them.

This is not necessarily a matter only of "balancing" needs and claims, for we may be willing to "go the extra mile" for the one we love or for the cause we have embraced. Nor is it to "take the heart out of" truly other-centered love (by a concern for our own selves), for we may be willing to lose ourselves for those we love. It can be a matter of contradiction in the very love we give. To violate some of these limits can destroy ourselves and the one we love. For if a certain way of living, of acting, of loving is indeed destructive of ourselves as persons, it cannot ultimately be good for the other who demands it of us. No person's good is achieved by the destruction of another person *as a person*, however much their needs and interests may conflict.

Many of our problems with the limits of self-sacrifice come in relationships marked by inequality, especially the inequality of power. The experience of self-sacrifice and the issues of self-love versus other-love are drastically influenced by the balance of power in a relationship. To ignore this fact in discussions of "rules of preference" or balance of obligations is to risk skewing the realities with which we are concerned. Thus, to a great extent what Ibsen's Nora and the feminists who have identified with her have cried out against is the expectation that women will be more self-sacrificial than men or that self-sacrificial subservient roles are as such self-fulfilling for those "born to them." When a disproportionate burden of sacrifice is laid on one person in a commitment-relationship, and when the person who bears it is the one with the least power, the duty of self-sacrifice is morally suspect. This suggests that where there is an imbalance of power, the expectation ought to be that the one with the greater power will be obligated to the greater self-sacrifice.

Limits to a just self-sacrifice do not disappear when we take account of the common good, the good of the wider community beyond the person or group to whom we are specifically committed. It is true that this wider good may make more stringent our obligations of fidelity, but it does not rule out totally the need to consider obligations to ourselves. Indeed, sometimes the social context, where even our most intimate relationships are pushed and pulled into patterns of dominance and subordination, forces upon us the problem of justice and fidelity to self as well as justice and fidelity to another.

All of these considerations may come together in the deeply moving example of the commitment of Prem Bodasingh, the young heroine of Alan Paton's *Ah, But Your Land Is Beautiful*. The brightest student in Durban, South Africa, she is arrested for sitting in the "No Blacks" section of the public library. No amount of persuasion by the Director of Education, who visits her in jail, can change her understanding of the requirements of fidelity. Her commitment leads her to seemingly total self-sacrifice, yet her fidelity is paradoxically to God and to her people but also to herself.

—Do you understand that you may be damaging your whole life?
—I understand it.
—Are you willing to throw away education, knowledge, learning, for the sake of your cause?

She said to him in a low voice,
—Yes.
—But these are—what shall I say—holy things.
She said with a spark of fire,
—The cause is holy too. And my promise. A promise is holy too.
—A promise to whom? To Congress?
—No. To God and myself.
—What was your promise, Prem? . . . .
—To the death.[21]

A Just Resolution

It may be enough to show, as I have tried to do, the *possibility* of release from a commitment-obligation when another obligation supersedes it. But how do we resolve these conflicts? How do we determine whether, when these sorts of conflicts emerge, we are indeed released from commitment-obligations? For the sheer fact of conflict does not lead to the conclusion that a commitment-obligation is overridden. After all, every conflict could require resolution in favor of the standing promise. Unless the conflict is between two promises already made (when the sheer impossibility of fulfilling both can release the obligation of one of them), the "overriding" of a commitment-obligation presumes another, more stringent, obligation. On what basis will we recognize this?

I have said that no one fundamental principle provides the solution to every conflict of this kind, and no ordering of principles (such as promise-keeping first, do no injury to others always second, and so on) settles every troubling case. The fundamental imperative of a just love tells us where to look and what to consider; it provides a focus for our discernment. But it demands, rather than provides by itself, a careful discernment of what is most respectful of and most in accord with the concrete reality of the persons involved.

There are ways in which traditional moral theory has attempted to deal with conflicts such as I have described, and it may be helpful to remind ourselves of some of them. As we saw in the previous chapter, some theorists have tried to adjudicate the multiple claims we experience by identifying a principle of *need* (Augustine's norm for giving time and attention to his congregation rather than to his friends). Others have made the determinative principle *proximity*, or the closeness of our relation to those who need our response (something suggested, for example, by Thomas Aquinas's argument that greater love is due those who are closer to us.[22] Still other theorists have combined these criteria with additional ones such as *last resort* (someone has a claim that only I can meet).[23]

Resolving conflicts in our multiple obligations can be a matter of distributive justice—the just allocation of our time and energy and resources. When it is, the principles of need, of proximity, of last resort, or of equality or equitable sharing, or a principle like the contemporary Christian formulation of a "preferential option for the poor," are extremely important and can be extremely helpful, for they do help us determine priorities in our choices.

But the conflicts I have been talking about are not always matters only of distributive justice. They involve not just determining who needs our care or our goods—our faithfulness in this sense. They involve our special obligations to particular persons because of our commitments. They involve justifying (or not) our release from the obligation to keep our word. They involve, then, not just determining how a principle of distributive justice will guide our decisions, but whether (for example) certain principles of distributive justice (such as equality, or priority on the basis of need) will ever take precedence over the principle of promise-keeping. Insofar as the problem is characterized in this way, it is more like the traditional problem of justifying a suspension of the principle of truth-telling (justified lying) or justifying a suspension of the principle requiring that we preserve human life (justifying, for example, cessation of life-support systems for a dying person, or justifying war). Traditional methods for dealing with situations in which such basic values conflict (for example, the method used in what is known as "just war theory") can be useful in resolving questions of commitment as well—however strange that may sound to our ears.[24]

But whatever methods we use to try to discern whether we are bound or released from the commitments we have made, the overall task is the same. We may resolve questions of obligation regarding our promised deeds of love by taking account of the seriousness and urgency of need (on the part of those who claim our action), the nature of the commitment-relationship, the implications for the common good, and so forth. We shall resolve the questions of radical obligation regarding whole frameworks for loving only when we determine what we shall love with an absolute love.

Chapter 8

Commitment, Covenant, and Faith

I said in the beginning of this book that our questions about commitment ultimately connect with our deepest religious and theological concerns. They are ultimately questions about basic beliefs and fundamental loves. I maintained, moreover, that understanding our experiences of commitment, of love, of obligation, and of fidelity would help us to understand our religious beliefs and to distinguish our loves. Now we must probe these possibilities, in however brief a way.

First, some general observations are important regarding the multiple influences of religion on concrete experiences of commitment. Some persons, of course, deem religious considerations irrelevant to the making and keeping of commitments. Religion, they say, cannot help us, and it should not be allowed to hinder. For others, however, religion is a key element in decisions about commitment. Like the potential uses of religion in every other area of human affairs, its power can be brought to bear on commitments in vastly different ways. It can be destructive and distortive of persons and relationships, or it can be creative and illuminating.

Sometimes, for example, religion (in whatever tradition) functions as a harsh reminder of duty, a source of fear and guilt, a tight vise holding us in the grip of the promises we have made. It raises the stakes of our commitments, for it seems to tell us that if we break them, not only do we fail, but we sin; and not only do we sin against one another, but we sin against God. By the same token, religion (or better, religious faith) can serve to free us from a compulsive sense of obligation; it offers us hope in forgiveness, or liberation from too narrow a view of our options. It can summon us to courage, to brave patience or bold action, to faithfulness that could be, but somehow is not, beyond our strength. When we mourn our incomplete lives, afraid that we shall never find the "end of ourselves" in the commitments we have made, sometimes we believe still, on religious grounds, in the essential openness of life to us. And sometimes when we do come to the "end of ourselves"—not, however, in the sense of glorious fulfillment but in the terrible prospect of death—through our commitments there is a divine faith that gives meaning to an ultimate surrender.

My chief concern in this chapter is neither to sort out the harmful uses of religion in relation to human commitments nor to provide a positive ground for particular forms of commitment. It is easy enough to deplore the appearance of religious scrupulosity in the keeping of promises but not so easy to discern whether our sense of obligation is irrational or simply honest and responsible. Likewise, it is possible to offer religious reasons for specific forms or frameworks of commitment, but another task altogether to sort out the cultural roots of religious beliefs about particular commitments (such as the belief still held by some that a Christian marriage includes an essential commitment to a patriarchal model of power relations between husband and wife).

What I do want to do is to examine connections between a religious tradition and the understandings of commitment I have been working with throughout the previous chapters. An obvious case in point is the Covenant tradition that the Jewish and Christian religions both affirm as integral to their faith. Here is a story of explicit promises made between God and human persons, promises to love and to do the deeds of love, to be present in love (indeed, to "abide" in it), and faithful through changes that unfold in time. The narratives and the prophetic interpretations of the Covenant in the Hebrew Bible proclaim God's unconditional commitment to a people, and they gradually clarify the nature of that people's struggle to understand and to sustain an absolute commitment to God. This story of the Covenant is reappropriated generation after generation in the traditions of Judaism and in the Christian communities of and beyond the New Testament. It offers a critically important perspective on the possibility of commitment and fidelity, and on aspects of commitment that are for us especially problematic. We need not make it the center of all biblical theology nor read it into every form of human commitment in order to glimpse in it new dimensions of commitment that transform the limits of what we have heretofore been able to consider.

It seems an obvious thing to do—to focus on the Covenant tradition in an exploration of commitment. Yet serious problems, even enormous pitfalls, beset such a move. The long history of the Covenant tradition's emergence and reapplication has been marked by countless contradictions, and any brief treatment of it today risks not only confusion but damage to individuals and to groups.

There are, first of all, many ways of interpreting the Covenant, and its meaning and even its importance are matters of debate for biblical scholars. As D. J. McCarthy observed, "Covenant is so important in the Scriptures that in the form of 'testament' it has provided the title for the book, but it is so complex an idea that we have our problems in understanding it."[1] The pieces of the plot do not fall neatly together in one recorded history. The Jewish and Christian communities whose story it is have told and retold it with conflicting memories and conflicting beliefs.

Moreover, the history of the Covenant's interpretation and of its use in different theologies shows an alarming potential for the oppression of groups and individuals—in spite of its remarkable possibilities for liberation and for life. Thus, for example, both Christians and Jews have been tempted to read ancient forms of the story into ongoing history in ways that have prevented acknowledgment of God's relation to people who are outside of particular forms of the Covenant tradition. Likewise, Christians have sometimes attempted to subordinate the "old" covenant to its fulfillment in the life and death of Jesus, and even to assert the abrogation of God's commitment to the Jews. In so doing, they have often manipulated and abused the Covenant tradition for mistaken or immoral purposes, including the overt persecution of the Jewish people. In the twentieth century the Holocaust has led at least some Christians to reject such interpretations, but it has also caused some Jews to question a tradition that could allow the acceptance of human atrocities as if from the hands of God or that could seem so counter-to-fact in terms of empirical evidence for God's fidelity to Israel. In addition to the scandals of anti-Semitism and religious chauvinism, and the contradictions of human history, feminists have identified other problems, such as the tradition's massive dependence on the imagery of lord-servant and husband-wife relationships.

Despite all of these difficulties, however, the Covenant tradition can, I believe, illuminate important aspects of commitment. If it is interpreted with sufficient caution, it retains a power to express the convictions of a fundamentally strengthening and freeing faith. The questions that implicitly guide us here include: (1) How does what is revealed through the Covenant tradition shed light on our general understanding of commitment? (2) How does our reflective analysis of our experience of commitment help us to understand what is revealed in the Covenant tradition? With these questions, and cautions in mind, let me attempt a theological and ethical interpretation of the Covenant tradition, one that locates at the heart of the available biblical testimony (and the ongoing internal witness of the communities of faith) an arguable set of truths of profound significance for human hopes of commitment.

THE MEANING OF THE COVENANT

Those who stand within the Covenant tradition must have assumed, or struggled to achieve, answers to questions such as: Has a covenant really been made? If so, by whom, and to whom, and with what content? And is the word that has been promised a word that can be trusted? As I have already said, the story of the Covenant, however difficult its meaning and varied its interpretations, is the story above all of God's commitment to human persons. It includes specific events in relation to which the biblical authors try to express an experience of God making promises, God giving God's word, to individuals and to a people. It also includes the story of the response of human persons to God. Out of the complexities of the Covenant narrative, certain key elements emerge—not without ambiguity or controversy in their articulation. The following formulations may begin to focus these elements in a way that can facilitate our consideration of their relevance to the problems of commitment.

1. God has made an unconditional commitment of unconditional love to human persons.
2. God's promise is addressed to human persons in a way that takes account of their reality as persons and that thereby calls for and makes possible a responding personal and communal commitment.
3. God is faithful to this promise.
4. God's word relativizes every framework of human commitment.
5. God's commitment makes possible the breaking of otherwise insurmountable barriers within and between persons, so that they can commit themselves to one another in some form of faithful love.
6. God's promise is given to persons *in via*, while they are not yet capable of perfect fidelity.

Each of these statements needs careful consideration, since each represents a claim that is not only complex but in some way debatable. I turn, then, first to the substance of the promise.

The Promise

God has made an unconditional commitment of unconditional love to human persons. Whether or not the Covenant is as dominant in the Hebrew and Christian scriptures as many biblical scholars have maintained, it is certainly a major theme. It may not be superfluous here to remind ourselves of some of its appearances. It is, in fact, sufficiently pervasive that some interpreters say it is implicit from the beginning of God's relationship with the world, in the acts of God as creator.[2] God "spread out the earth upon the waters . . . [God's] steadfast love endures for ever" (Ps. 136:6). The decision to create already includes a commitment to maintain what is created. But the story of the relationship between God and what God creates unfolds into particular moments (metaphorical or real) when God is said to speak explicit promises and to make formal covenants.

To Noah and all humanity who come after him, God pledges: "Here is the sign of the covenant which I make between me and you and every living creature that is with you, for all future generations: I set my bow in the clouds" (Gen. 9:12–13). Generations upon generations later, God promises to Abraham: "I will establish my covenant between me and you and your descendants after you throughout their generations for an everlasting covenant, to be God to you and to your descendants after you" (Gen. 17:7–8). The descendants of Abraham and Sarah become, then, the "bearers of the promise." When they are enslaved in a foreign land under a hostile ruler, God hears their "groaning," leads them out into the Sinai desert, and covenants with them anew through Moses. "The Lord our God made a covenant with us in Horeb. Not with our ancestors did the Lord make this covenant, but with us, who are all of us here alive today . . . face to face at the mountain, out of the midst of the fire . . . [God] said: 'I am the Lord your God, who brought you out of the land of Egypt, out of the house of bondage. You shall have no other gods before me'" (Deut. 5:2–7).

Centuries later, the monarchy of King David is marked by yet another experience of the Covenant. The prophet Nathan brings to David the word of God: "I will appoint a place for my people Israel. . . . [T]he Lord will make you a house" (2 Sam. 7:10–12). Under Solomon, David's son, the nation divides into two kingdoms, both of which sustain political and military threats, and final defeat. The people are forced into exile. During the long years that follow, the experience of the Covenant is kept alive through the voice of the prophets. They cry to God to remember God's people, and they cry to the people to remember the promises of God. The Covenant forms the people's identity and challenges their love; it also offers their only hope. "Incline your ear, and come to me; hear, that your soul may live; and I will make with you an everlasting covenant, my steadfast, sure love for David" (Isa. 55:3). "I will put my law within them, and I will write it upon their hearts; and I will be their God, and they shall be my people. . . . [T]hey shall all know me, from the least of them to the greatest" (Jer. 31:33–34). However many forms the Covenant takes throughout the history of ancient

Israel, and however many biblical theologies inform the people's understanding of the Covenant, a narrative kernel goes forward, affirming that God has given God's word: "I will be your God, and you shall be my people."

When the great schism of Christianity from Judaism takes place, belief in the Covenant continues in the new movement as in the older religion. The early Christian community, trying to understand its experience in continuity with God's promises to Israel, looks to the scriptures for an explanation of its ongoing faith and hope. Christians see their own story as a sequel to the Hebrew Bible's story of the Covenant. God's commitment through Jesus, they believe, is a continuation and confirmation of the Covenant given to Abraham, Moses, and David and spoken of by the prophets. Thus, the gospel writers appeal to the images of the Covenant when they describe the words of Jesus to his disciples at their last Passover meal: "This is my blood of the covenant, which is poured out for many" (Mk. 14:24; also Lk. 22:19–20 and Matt. 26:28). And under the image of the Spirit of God, the covenant relationship is sustained through yet another promise, the promise of the Holy Spirit: "I shall ask God, and you will be given another Advocate to be with you forever" (Jn. 14:16).

Many Christians, of course, have held the view that Jesus (as Messiah) constitutes the fulfillment of the Covenant as it was predicted in the Hebrew Scriptures. Given this rendering, the role of Israel can be restricted to the mere transmission of the messianic promises. The writings of Paul, however, offer a different perspective, for "the gifts and the call of God are irrevocable" (Rom. 11:29). As the New Testament scholar Nils Dahl has argued, Paul does not believe that the life and death of Jesus *fulfilled* the Covenant (though Jesus did fulfill the scriptures in important ways). "On the contrary, Jesus' work *reaffirmed* the commitment of the god who is faithful."[3] According to Paul, the Covenant of the Hebrew scriptures is not a prediction, but a pledge of ongoing relationship. "For I tell you that Christ became a servant of the circumcised to show God's truthfulness, in order to confirm the promises given to the patriarchs, and in order that the Gentiles might glorify God for [God's] mercy" (Rom. 15:8–9).

The substance of the Covenant, as Paul interprets it, is this: "I will live in them and move among them, and I will be their God and they shall be my people" (2 Cor. 6:16). It is this that is ratified, confirmed, and opened to the Gentiles by the incarnation, ministry, and death of Jesus. "For all the promises of God find their Yes in him" (2 Cor. 1:20). God's word is given in Jesus Christ, and it is sealed in a radical way through Jesus' death. Yet it is a word that continues to be given in pledge, over and over again, through the Spirit of God. In Jesus Christ, says Paul, the Covenant is "sealed with the promised Holy Spirit, which is the guarantee of our inheritance until we acquire possession of it" (Eph. 1:13–14). Moreover, the ministry of Paul and of the church is not simply a report of the fulfillment of the Covenant but part of its ongoing process. "Remember it is God who assures us all, and you, of our standing in Christ, and has anointed us, marking us with [God's] seal and giving us the pledge, the Spirit, that we carry in our hearts" (2 Cor. 1:21–22, Jerusalem Bible). From this Christian perspective, then, what is begun with creation, renewed and specified with Abraham and Sarah, with Moses and David and the prophets, is carried into the Word "made flesh" and finally the pledge of the Spirit.

If we ponder the story of the Covenant in the light of our previous reflections on the nature of commitment, of love, of fidelity, it seems appropriate to speak of it in these terms: What is given in the Covenant is always God's word. The word is backed, it is true, by "mighty deeds": offspring are conceived in old women; slaves are liberated from hopeless bondage; people lost and wandering in a desert are finally led home; one who dies is raised from the dead. Yet God does not always do the deeds that are expected, even when they are desperately needed. Often, as it is recorded by the biblical authors, what the people seem to have is only God's word. It rings through their memory of God's power and God's care, but it is still fundamentally a word given in promise, sealed in covenant. Yielded to the people in this way, the word dwells with them. Their struggle is to believe in it. But what does it promise? Of what does it give them assurance? To what does it give them a claim?

The promise is ultimately always a promise of a relationship, a promise of unconditional love and ongoing presence. "I will be your

God. You shall be my people." Here the word given is not merely a verbal report, not merely an intellectual affirmation. Here is the performative word of commitment, what we have seen before as the "'real' in the speaker, begotten, spoken, first in the heart."[4] Through and in this word, God abides with this people. The understanding of what this means changes as different aspects of human life become important at different times. Thus, it is identified in the people's minds with land and progeny in the covenant with Abraham, with liberation and refuge in the Mosaic covenant, with peace and order in the covenant with David, with wisdom and justice in the prophetic traditions after the exile, with a new kingdom in the coming of Jesus. What remains the same, however, through these changing interpretations of the meaning of the Covenant, is the promise of ongoing unconditional love. And in the ongoing love lies the promise of a future, of a realm of justice and the ultimate conquest of death. Though appearances may be to the contrary, and though the people's voices may grow hoarse with crying for a new manifestation of the word, God's love and the care it entails are never revoked.

If we probe even more deeply this interpretation of the Covenant (bringing to bear the concepts that emerged in our earlier exploration of commitment), an amazing story is here: God, in truth, gives God's word—yields a claim over God's own promised actions, disposes God's own self in a new way, "places" God's self in and among human persons, dwells with them through a binding commitment. Promises are made, we have seen, to strengthen the shakable wills of those who make them and to provide assurance to those who receive them. If God has no need to be strengthened in intention and fidelity, human persons nonetheless have need of assurance of this. The form of the Covenant provides them with a means for just such assurance—revealing, as it does, God's "settled decision" in their regard.

Given any continuity of concepts at all between our general understanding of commitment and the possible meanings of the Covenant, what can be said of the Covenant? God's commitment to human persons is such that if God needed a claim placed on the love that is pledged (in order to be strengthened in the love), human persons would have such a claim; for the word of God is entrusted to them. Given any continuity of concepts at all between our general understanding of love and the possible meanings of God's love for human persons, what can we say of God's love? God's very being is placed in affirmation of the being of human persons—utterly creative (unlike human love) but also responsive and unitive. And given any continuity of concepts between our general understanding of fidelity and the meaning of God's own faithfulness, what can be said of God's fidelity? God abides with human persons, present to them in a shared history, holding together the past of the Covenant and the future it promises.

All of this, however, makes more urgent the kinds of questions that the Covenant tradition has always generated—questions of the conditionality of God's pledges, of particularity in God's choices, of the compatibility of tragedy with continuing human trust in the God of the Covenant. These are questions of the limits to God's promises and God's love, and they cannot be ignored if we are to try to understand the relevance of the Covenant to our own possibilities of commitment and love.

The Response

God's promise is addressed to human persons in a way that takes account of their reality as persons, and that thereby calls for and makes possible a responding personal and communal commitment. The story of the Covenant, of course, is the story not only of God's commitment to human persons but also of the commitment of human persons to God. An adequate interpretation of this side of the Covenant leads quickly and deeply into theologies of grace and salvation, divine election and human freedom. I cannot here follow this lead (any more than I can move in these brief considerations into the whole of the doctrine of God that is implied in interpreting God's pledges to humanity). What is necessary in the present context, however, is some reflection on the manner in which the Covenant depends on the participation of human persons. Along with this will come some understanding of the nature of this participation.

The story of the Covenant, I have said, is the story of God's unconditional promise of an everlasting love. But might it still be maintained that God's promise to the people of Israel and to the followers of Jesus is in some way a conditional promise after all?

No one would maintain, of course, that the promise is conditional in the sense that changed circumstances can stretch God's fidelity beyond God's strength, or that God rests the Covenant on essentially conditioned "qualities" in human persons. However, an argument might be made that God does indeed stipulate one condition, one term, on the fulfillment of which depends God's willingness to sustain the Covenant. This condition is simply that the Israelites obey the Law and that Christians fulfill the requirements of Christian love. It is this condition, in fact, that is often the basis for differentiating the Mosaic covenant from the covenants made with Abraham and with David. On Mount Sinai, the message is given through Moses: "You have seen what I did to the Egyptians, and how I bore you on eagles' wings and brought you to myself. Now, therefore, *if you will obey my voice and keep my covenant*, you shall be my own possession among all peoples; for all the earth is mine" (Exod. 19:4–6, italics mine). And except where Christianity has affirmed an unyielding doctrine of predestination, has it not been considered possible for individuals to fall out of the Covenant-relation? Paul, for example, may not have considered obedience to the law a condition for participation in the new Covenant, but he does make faith an absolute requirement.

Is God's commitment, therefore, conditional or unconditional? Can human refusal or betrayal of the Covenant be significant enough that God's promise will be withdrawn? Is the last word in the Covenant story as likely to be judgment and rejection as it is to be forgiveness? And if the last word is forgiveness, will it be so only if God ignores, or transcends, the very "terms" of the Covenant?

The answers to such questions must not come too easily. We could perhaps try to resolve them by appealing to something like what Phyllis Trible calls the "pilgrimage of an ancient portrait of God"—a portrait that holds together a view of God as pledging love and as also promising judgment and justice.[5] There is another way I would like to explore, however, a way that seeks to understand how it is that God does not ultimately withdraw from the Covenant *even though* there are expectations and requirements for human response.

First it is necessary to remember that both the Hebrew and Christian scriptures portray overall a God whose desire is a relationship with human persons, whose commitment to this is renewed again and again, and who in fact professes often to love with an unconditional love. The story of the Covenant is ultimately one of a God who does *not* withdraw divine promises or presence, despite every provocation. On Sinai, for example, the Covenant is no sooner made than it is violated (for a golden idol is fashioned to take the place of God), but no sooner violated than renegotiated (Exod. 32–34). Judgment may be given, injustice decried, but God does not abandon the Covenant. Sometimes God's forgiveness goes so far it overwhelms, wipes out, the people's sins. "[God] does not retain anger for ever, because [God] delights in steadfast love. [God] will again have compassion upon us [and] tread our iniquities under foot" (Mic. 7:18–19). God even sets an example for human persons in this regard: "Love your enemies, . . . and you will be [children] of the Most High; for [God] is kind to the ungrateful and the selfish" (Lk. 6:35). But why? Are the "terms" of the Covenant then arbitrary? Is the ongoing tension between God's justice and mercy merely a ploy? *Does it make any difference at all what human persons do in response to God's promise?*

In one sense, it makes no difference. God's love is committed to human persons unconditionally. It is expressed unconditionally to the people of Israel in countless ways and times, and this same commitment can be said to be sealed irrevocably in and by the death of Jesus.[6] Once a commitment is made and lived "unto death," there can be no turning back. It cannot be undone or withdrawn. No, God's love is not pledged conditionally. Whatever the response of human persons, the love and the promise remain.

But in another sense, what human persons do in response to God's promise makes, indeed, all the difference in the world. In fact, God seems (according to the Covenant story) to have gone to great lengths to insist that this does make a difference—both to the world and to God. But what sort of difference can it make, if the commitment of God does not depend on it? The response of human persons can make a difference only if there is something about the *goal* of the Covenant that cannot be realized without it. That is, human response can make a serious difference only if the goal of the Covenant (and of God's love) includes a relationship that is mutual and if mutuality between God and human persons depends on the free response of human persons. Just as it is always possible for any one person to choose (unilaterally and unconditionally) to *love* another, but not possible for that person unilaterally to choose *friendship* with the other (since friendship requires a responding mutual love), so it is possible for God to commit God's own love unconditionally, but not to effect friendship (mutuality) with human persons without their response.

The goal of the Covenant appears indeed to include a relationship that is mutual. The offer is the offer of communion—of being known and knowing, being loved and loving. This is the offer of a God whose glory is manifest in shared history, shared labor, but also in shared intimacy with the people God creates. And God's desire for response seems to be an anguished yearning as often as it is a command. The only response that will suffice (the condition for the fulfillment of the Covenant) is for human persons to love God with their whole heart and soul and mind and strength. The whole point of the Law is to guide such a response; and the requirements of discipleship are the requirements of this response. The essential "terms" of the Covenant are not rules extrinsic to its life; they are formative of the relationship that is its goal.

The Covenant, then, is addressed to human persons in their concrete reality *as persons*. It takes account of their relationality (their capacity and need for union by knowledge and by love) and their freedom (their capacity and responsibility for self-determination).[7] It offers them what "eye has not seen, nor ear heard," beyond the possible expectations of humanity, but not beyond its possible grace. It does so in a way that asks of them an unconditional commitment to an absolute love.

Divine Fidelity

God is faithful to the promise. An explanation of the conditionality that is compatible with the unconditionality of God's commitment does not by itself solve all problems of human trust in the Covenant.

For when a covenant is made unconditionally, there remains the question of whether or not it will be kept—in this case, whether or not God is and will be faithful to the Covenant once made.

The issue of trust in God's fidelity is critical for anyone who stands within the Covenant tradition. Presumably those who stake their lives on God's word have a great deal to lose should the word prove false or fickle. They may be risking everything, whether they flee across the Red Sea or cast their lot with the disciples of a marked man. They court despair if they place their ultimate hope in a God who hides from them when they expect presence or who abandons them when they expect help. More than this, only belief in a God who is utterly lovable and totally trustworthy can draw human persons to an absolute love. Short of such a belief, they will do well at most to obey, or to negotiate with, a powerful being who is untrustworthy or unjust.

The problem is a real one, for it is the problem of the human experience of suffering. In the context of the Covenant tradition, however, it takes on a special form. It is the suffering of God-forsakenness. Stories are multiplied in the biblical history of God's relationship with individuals and peoples—stories that Phyllis Trible calls "texts of terror" and James Crenshaw describes as a "whirlpool of torment."[8] They are tales in which the characters know a "sense of personal betrayal and outrage,"[9] or we know it for them as we interpret their plight and behold again their agony. God's actions in their regard seem to contradict all God's pledged intentions and revealed desires. God appears not only as one who does not fulfill what is promised but as one who abandons, uses, excludes, conspires against, defeats, hands over to be raped and killed. Sometimes the stories are ironical for us, because we know the outcome finally proves God's faithfulness. But it is not always so. Isaac is saved (though Abraham seems cruelly manipulated), and Job glimpses his vindicator and feels the presence of God. But Hagar is forever excluded, and the daughter of Jephtha is dead and almost forgotten.

We need not look only to the tragedies of the biblical narratives to understand this suffering, however. As Trible says, the tales of terror go on. They go on in individual lives and in the lives of peoples; they are a part of humanity's story. And through them still runs the dread of divine forsakenness, the cry of the heart that fears it is betrayed. How shall we interpret the evidence that points to God's inconstancy? What can be answered to the bitter complaint, "God breaks me down on every side, and I am gone, and my hope God has pulled up like a tree"? (Job 19:10). What response can be given when "a voice is heard in Ramah, lamentation and bitter weeping; Rachel is weeping for her children; she refuses to be comforted for her children, because they are not"? (Jer. 31:15). What explanation can be offered to a people whose faithfulness seems sometimes surer than the faithfulness of God?

There are some answers that will not help, some explanations that will not suffice unless we want to deny completely the demands of religious and moral reason. We cannot, for example, rest content with the solution (offered sometimes even by the biblical authors) that God is simply "testing" individuals and communities through misfortune and apparent abandonment. At least in some senses of the term, God has no need to test what is in the heart of human persons (for God knows inmost thoughts and commitments); a trustworthy God will not "play games" with persons, not set up hurdles for the sake of having them crossed. Pierre Teilhard de Chardin, reflecting on the experience of God's hiddenness and silence, observes that

> to justify this obscurity, so strangely incompatible with the divine sun, scholars explain that the Lord deliberately hides himself in order to test our love. One has to be hopelessly lost in intellectual games, or never to have encountered either in oneself or others the sufferings of doubt, not to see what is detestable in such an answer. O my God, your creatures stand before you, lost and in anguish, appealing for your help. To have them rush to you, it would be enough to show them a single ray of your light, the fringe of your coat—and you would not do this for them?[10]

There may be a sense in which, as we saw in regard to human growth in fidelity,[11] the experience of absence can allow an experience of greater presence, and terrible suffering—if it does not destroy us—can reveal to us our own capacities to love, hollow out our hearts, challenge our imaginations, and actually help us to love with integrity and greathearted courage. But suffering may not yield this result *unless* we can trust in a just and faithful God.

It will also not be sufficient, then, to reduce seemingly grave moral contradictions (on God's part) to phases in a process that leads to an overall good. For if God is just, God cannot violate persons *as persons* any more than humans can justifiably destroy themselves or one another as persons. This may seem to measure God's actions in human terms, to forget that "God's ways are not our ways." Whatever the radical differences between divine and human ways, however, it cannot be (if God is to be trusted) that God's ways are *less just* than human ways. That is to say, a God faithful to God's promises cannot deal with human persons in ways that are arbitrary, or that come from evil motives, or that exploit persons for the sake of twisted needs on God's part.

In fact, both Jewish and Christian conceptions of God affirm that God's justice is *intelligible* to human persons. As Ronald Green points out, nowhere is this made clearer in the Jewish tradition than in the divine command to Israel (Lev. 19:2) that the people must model their behavior on the ways of God.[12] The God who is to be imitated is a just God—manifesting universal concern, impartiality, fairness, faithfulness, and an abhorrence of cheating, deceit, oppression, and vengeance. Moreover, God is a merciful God—going beyond (not falling short of) justice through divine forbearance, patience, and willingness to forgive.[13] Similar calls to love and to act on the model of God's action can be found in the Christian gospel, whether in the injunction "You, therefore, must be perfect, as God is perfect" (Matt. 5:48), or in the pattern that the Gospel of John attributes to Jesus: "As God has loved me, so I have loved you" (Jn. 15:9), and "I have given you an example so that you may copy what I have done to you" (Jn. 13:15).

If it is unacceptable to explain the experience of God-forsakenness only in terms of a divine testing or in terms of contradictions in God's intentions, what *can* we say, finally, about the faithfulness of

God to the Covenant? The tales of terror may continue, and the whirlpools of torment may never be completely stilled. If we cannot explain them away, is there enough evidence, or are there sufficient reasons—either in the Covenant story itself or in the broader experience of human persons—to provide grounds for trust in a word that is pledged by God?

The memory of those who stand within the Covenant is primarily a memory of the *faithful* deeds of God. They remember a God who saved them from slavery, who remained with them despite their own forgetfulness or faithlessness, who formed them into a people and who continues to be their God. They remember a God who dwelt among them and who makes a home with them by the power of God's own Spirit. It may be that their memory slips from time to time, that it finds ways to forget the counterevidence, to ignore the moments of tragedy and despair. Yet even here, deep within this memory, there is a witness to God's fidelity. For at least some of those who were "tested," whose voices were reduced to silence or raised in terrible cries of abandonment, did not finally give testimony of despair. Abraham, Jeremiah, Job, Rachel—their stories all say, finally, that God was with them, not against them; that there was a future for them and for their people; that *the Covenant held.* "I know that my Redeemer lives" (Job 19:25). "Keep your voice from weeping, and your eyes from tears. . . . There is hope for your future, says the Lord" (Jer. 31:16). "Call to me and I will answer you, and will tell you great and hidden things which you have not known" (Jer. 33:3).

When we try to make sense of this, we move in several directions. Like Teilhard de Chardin, sometimes we look to a process—and see in it not God's use of persons as mere means but the gradual unfolding of new possibilities for all.

No, God does not hide himself to make us search for him, of that I am sure—much less to let us suffer in order to increase our merits. On the contrary, bent down over his creation which moves upwards to him, he works with all his power to give us happiness and light. Like a mother he watches over his newly born child. But our eyes are unable to see him yet. Is not precisely the whole course of centuries needed in order for our gaze to accustom itself to the light?[14]

Sometimes this means that the Covenant itself is reinterpreted, as the prophets try to understand its meaning during the exile. When Jerusalem falls and the land is lost, when the monarchy is destroyed and the people are dislocated, faith struggles to understand the faithfulness of God.[15] Sometimes it is only from a temporal distance that believers in the Covenant glimpse not only God's justice but God's mercy in a love that lets bodies be destroyed, minds ravaged, spirits crushed, and that does not hinder the cry, "Why have you forsaken me?"

Above all there may come the recognition that the tragedies of life are not manufactured for human persons by God, that the horror that besets individuals and groups is not of God's making.[16] Before this recognition comes the awareness that the process of life is one not only of growth but also of struggle against the forces of evil. What human persons do to one another, what human structures of violence perpetuate in the human community—these are not from the hand of God. And a commitment on the part of any persons (even if, and perhaps because, they are participants in the Covenant) to oppose the forces of evil can lead them not only to great suffering but even to the point of death.

The strongest evidence that the Covenant tradition has for not implicating God in fundamentally evil actions and for not blaming God for human tragedy is the evidence that God somehow takes on God's own self the burden of human suffering. "The biblical testimony to a God who suffers along with and because of humans is eloquent indeed."[17] In Judaism, God is portrayed as suffering with those who suffer (so that suffering can in this way be a sign of personal favor with God). In Christian belief, the story unfolds radically into the suffering and death of Jesus.

In the Covenant story, too, and in the ongoing experience of the Covenant communities, there are moments when life is new, when death seems overcome. There are inklings of a joy that is eternally sorrow-consoled and of a transformation that bursts the bonds of every expected limitation. The Christian experience of the resurrection of Jesus provides a radical ground for hope that every experience of God-forsakenness has begun to be transformed: The Covenant can hold against whatever forces of destruction; the God who seems to abandon is the God who ultimately saves.

There is evidence then—or at least testimony—that God is faithful. And where the evidence is missing and the testimony silent, reasons can be given that help to make plausible a continuing belief in the fidelity of God. There are limits, of course, to the answers that Judaism and Christianity give to the terrors of God-forsakenness. Even if the Covenant tradition could provide a fully satisfactory solution at a universal abstract level, human persons would not be spared the labor and the dread of looking for individual answers in their own concrete experience. But, finally, we should not be surprised that, as in relation to every other promise, anyone who trusts in God's Covenant must take the word of the one who gives it. The word that is trusted in this case is the pledge of a relationship that will not destroy, a justice that will reach to all, a love that is "stronger than death." The trust itself implies: "The grass withers, the flower fades; but the word of our God will stand forever" (Isa. 40:8).

The Covenant and Its Frameworks

God's word relativizes every framework of human commitment. I have already considered in several different contexts the role of "frameworks" for commitment.[18] What I have tried to make clear is that while our most significant commitments are commitments to love, we hardly ever commit ourselves simply to love. For the sake of our love (to stabilize it, express it, embody it in a form that will make ongoing demands upon us and allow us to share the lives of those we love) we almost always commit ourselves to certain frameworks for living out our love. The frameworks, then, take their whole meaning (at least originally) from the love they are meant to serve. Hence, when a framework for love no longer serves the love (and may even threaten it), the obligation we have to the framework may no longer hold. This is to say that commitments to frameworks are all relative to the love they are meant to serve. As relative, they may be essential to the love, or not. Our faithfulness depends on our discernment of the essential or nonessential connection of the frameworks to the love.

There is an aspect of the Covenant tradition that is especially relevant to the question of "frameworks" for love. I refer here to the Law, which is associated with the Covenant made with Moses at Sinai. Without adjudicating the multiple issues shared and joined by Jews and Christians regarding the relation of the Law to the Covenant, the debates offer some distinctions that help to illuminate the relation of all frameworks to a fundamental commitment to love. The crucial distinction, of course, lies in the question of whether the Law belongs to the substance of the Covenant or whether it is itself a "framework" that serves the substance by giving it form, nurturing it, guiding it, providing its expression. If and insofar as it is a framework for the substance of the Covenant, the question leads to a further distinction: whether the Law can be separated from the Covenant or whether its connection to the Covenant is essential.

It is clear that according to the biblical narrative the Law is incorporated into the Covenant at Sinai. What is debated is whether it is incorporated as something constitutive of, or subordinate to, the central substance of the Covenant. Paul's interpretation (which has influenced, though not completely dominated, much of Christian theology in this regard) is that the Law is separate from the substance of the Covenant and subordinate to it.[19] The Law, unlike the Covenant, has no power to give life. Its function is to reveal sin and the powerlessness of human persons in the face of their own sin. What is needed, and given in Jesus Christ, is a ratification of the Covenant first made with Abraham. What is required in response is only faith, now in Jesus Christ.

The common Jewish view, on the other hand (and one shared in part by some Christians), is that the Law is indeed a lifegiving gift from God. As such it is integral to the Covenant, the "constitutive act by which the Sinai covenant was ratified."[20] It provides the form of the people's response to God, making the Covenant mutual. It constitutes the content of the Covenant insofar as it is the embodiment of God's will on earth. It cannot be separated from faith, for the Torah is not an objectifiable entity independent of the actual relationship of human persons to God.[21]

My concern is not to reconcile the opposing positions in this debate. In my view, both the Pauline interpretation of the Law and certain tendencies in Judaism regarding the Law present serious difficulties. Moreover, the debate is all too often skewed because of misleading caricatures (based on Pauline statements about the Law) of Pharisaic Judaism on the one hand and controversies within Judaism itself over the meaning of the Law on the other hand. Further confusion arises because the Jewish concept of Torah is usually more comprehensive in its content than Christian concepts of the Law. However, what I want to consider here, against the background of this debate, is the question of the relation of "laws" (or what might be called the "framework") of commitment to what I have been calling the substance of the commitment—in this case, the "law" (or the obligation that is undertaken) precisely to love.

First of all, there may be something to be learned from the structure of the Sinai Covenant itself. Comparing the Covenant formulary with the formularies of ancient treaties, scholars identify four features in the formulation provided in Exodus 19:3–8.[22] There is *a preamble*, the function of which is to introduce God as the one who speaks. This is followed by an overview of the *prior history of the relationship* between God and this people: "You have seen what I did to the Egyptians, and how I bore you on eagles' wings and brought you to myself." Exodus 19:5–7 then provides *a statement of the substance* of the relationship that will form the Covenant: "If you will obey my voice and keep my covenant, you shall be my own possession among all peoples; for all the earth is mine, and you shall be to me a kingdom of priests and a holy nation." And included in the substance is the consent of the people: "So Moses came and called the elders of the people, and set before them all these words which the Lord had commanded him. And all the people answered together and said, 'All that the Lord has spoken we will do.'" *Specific stipulations*, the laws, come only after this (though they are reported as part of the total Covenant, as becomes clear in Exodus 20).[23]

Insofar as this analysis of the structure of the Covenant is accurate, it portrays the subordinate status of the Law in relation to the substance of the Covenant. Its tenuousness, however, leads us to another kind of analysis. The substance of the Covenant is the mutual commitment by God and human persons to love with a particular love. The fundamental Law of the Covenant is above all, then, the obligation to this love. Insofar as the "summary" of all other laws associated with the Covenant can be expressed in the words of Deuteronomy 6:5, "You shall love the Lord your God with all your heart and with all your soul, and with all your might," and the words of Leviticus 19:18, "You shall love your neighbor as yourself," the Law belongs to the substance of the Covenant. But the specifications of the Law (that is, the "laws") are *for the sake of* the substance, for the sake of the love that is promised and obligated.

If the Law in the sense of the many laws associated with the Covenant is *for the sake of* the substance of the Covenant, how are they meant to serve it? Some laws formulate the requirements of a just love. They specify, for instance, what is necessary if love is to correspond to the concrete reality of human persons. The clearest example of this is in the Ten Words, the Decalogue. A just love of persons requires that they not be deceived, or killed, or robbed, and so on. Fundamental general laws like this are not the substance of the Covenant, but they are essential to it. For the love that is promised cannot be faithfully given unless it is given justly.

Other laws serve the substance of the Covenant by requiring observance of conditions that are conducive to fidelity; they nurture the "conditions of presence." Their purpose is "to fabricate a system of life in which restraint, self-discipline, and the tendency to relate every facet of human existence, however apparently inconsequential, to the will of God become a matter of instinct."[24]

Specific stipulations are, then, integral to the Covenant. Some of them are even essential. But they are *relative* to the central substance of the Covenant. Their purpose is to teach the ways of love, to aid in the discipline of a just love, to foster a community of justice and love. To forget them is to lose their wisdom and to forfeit their strength. "There is no faithfulness or kindness, and no knowledge of God in the land;

there is swearing, lying, killing, stealing, and committing adultery; they break all bounds and murder follows murder" (Hos. 4:1–2). To escalate the importance of these stipulations (or to confuse the inessential with the essential) is to be distracted by them, to make of them a barrier rather than a path to intimacy and a new creation. "Is not this the fast that I choose: to loose the bonds of wickedness, to undo the thongs of the yoke, to let the oppressed go free?" (Isa. 58:6).

The Covenant tradition therefore dramatizes what we have seen before: Frameworks take their meaning from the love they are designed to serve. They are relative in meaning and in value to the substance they help to frame. The obligation to sustain a framework or any part of it depends on its necessity to, or its support of, the love.

The Covenant Shared

God's commitment makes possible the breaking of otherwise insurmountable barriers within persons and between them, so that they can commit themselves to one another in some form of faithful love. The Covenant story has never been a story only of the relation between God and the individual soul. Indeed, an understanding of the dignity of the individual came later in the Covenant tradition than the understanding of identity in community. As we have seen, the promise was always understood to extend at least to the descendants of the one who received it. It pointed toward and constituted God's relation to a people. Its fundamental law irrevocably connected communion with God with union among persons. The Covenant of the Israelites with God was what enabled them to become a people. And Christian conceptions of the Covenant, too, are essentially communal. Indeed, the Eucharist (what might be called the central covenantal celebration for Christians) makes inseparable a commitment to God and a commitment to human persons.

But can the Covenant tradition help us with our understandings of commitment in human community? One way to test its relevance is to ask about three issues that may be especially problematic in this regard. These are the issues of (1) universality, (2) equality in mutuality, and (3) responsibility in relation to the world. In other words:

(1) Does the fact that God covenants with a particular community present a model for commitment between human persons that is fundamentally exclusive? (2) Does the covenant relation between God and human persons present a model for relations among human persons that negates the importance of equality in mutuality? (3) Can a covenant whose central substance is a relationship ("I will be your God, and you shall be my people") ground not only hope in, but human responsibility for, fashioning a better world? Once again, all that I can do here is to point to what constitute major questions for, for example, doctrines of the church, theologies of liberation, and religious ethics.

Universality

There is much in the story of the Covenant that would lead us to conclude that special relations with particular persons or groups are essentially exclusive. Insofar as the tradition bespeaks this point of view, it offers little help to those who are convinced that the goal of human love is a universal love of all persons or that the model for human relations ought to be an inclusive one. The Covenant story in the Hebrew scriptures is the story of God's special choice of a particular people. The relationship God forms with them is unique and intimate and one that gives them a special role in history. Christians, too, have sometimes claimed a special election by God in the ongoing Covenant confirmed in Jesus Christ. This special election has sometimes implied an arbitrary abandonment (by God) of those not chosen and a justification of colonization (by Christians) of those not yet among the elect.

All of this notwithstanding, the Covenant tradition contains a strong impetus toward an inclusive understanding of community and a universal form of human love. At the very least it can be said that there are within it important resources for such a view. In Christianity, for example, there exists a deep belief that the Covenant does not limit God's care to a particular nation or group. And at the heart of Christian understandings of morality is the command of a universal love of neighbor. Jesus' response to the question, "Who is my neighbor?" leaves little doubt that the weight of obligation is toward a love that opens to all and responds especially to need wherever it appears.

Moreover, it is a mistake to contrast Christian universalism with Jewish particularism in any way that suggests a less than universal concern on the part of Jews. Indeed, Jewish interpreters of the Covenant have often insisted, for example, that the special relation between God and the Jewish people reveals the relation between God and all humanity: God is the one God of all the nations; God's special care for Israel motivates divine compassion for all the universe; the wisdom of God reaches to every heart and every land; the particular bond between God and Israel opens to an eschatological hope for the gathering of all as one.[25] In addition, the Covenant itself places upon Jews a specific obligation to respect and care for the alien: "The stranger who sojourns with you shall be to you as the native among you, and you shall love [them] as yourself; for you were strangers in the land of Egypt" (Lev. 19:34).

What the Covenant tradition cannot be made legitimately to support is exaggerated individualism or communal isolationism. Challenges to these forms of human relation and commitment have multiplied from many sources. Today's needs remain acute, however, for an understanding of commitment that sees no opposition in principle between special relations and universal love, and between distinctive community values and concern for the whole human community. These needs may in fact be well served by the resources in the Covenant tradition. Here are at least possibilities to be tried: communal relations that respect the dignity of the individual; global relations that respect the values and structures of unique communities; particular relations that remain open circles and that form human hearts for wider and deeper loves.

Insofar as the Covenant points to possibilities for both universality and particularity in human relations, it highlights once more the importance of God's love as a model for love between humans. This is crucial again for reflection on issues of mutuality and equality in human relations.

Equality in Mutuality

We have already seen that mutuality is a concept central to the Covenant tradition because God's commitment to human persons has mutuality as its goal. But ought this mutuality serve as a model for key relationships in human lives? There is, of course, no doubt that it *has* so served, for it is commonplace in both Judaism and Christianity to pattern relations in society, the family, and the church on interpretations of the relation between God and human persons. The model as it has been interpreted has been perhaps most often the model of a transcendent God in relation to a submissive people. It suits the basic metaphor of the Mosaic covenant—the suzerainty treaty between overlord and vassal.[26] Historically these patterns, then, have tended to be ones of superiority and subordination, command and obedience, initiative and response, setting the terms of the Covenant and accepting them. But can it be that human persons are to establish all of their most significant committed relationships on a model in which one (in patriarchal systems, a husband, or a pastor, or a physician, or a statesman, and so forth) holds power over another in these ways?

There is no question that these patterns of relationship include reciprocity or a kind of mutuality that need not imply equality. There may be no question that they also include respect for the freedom of each party—as God respects the freedom of human persons in offering them participation in the Covenant. But the contribution of each, in such patterns, is different and unequal—one active perhaps, the other passive; one with power, the other subordinate. As patterns for human relationships, then, they no longer withstand the critique made of them by, for example, Jewish and Christian feminists. Without offering here a complete ethic for such relationships, two alternatives are possible. The Covenant model can be rejected or it can be differently interpreted. Let me suggest possibilities for the second.

First, it is necessary to clarify the content and the function of the model. Insofar as God's love is universal, for all human persons; insofar as it respects the concrete reality of persons in their freedom, their life in the world, and so on; insofar as it aims at mutuality as such; insofar as it offers an unconditional love that will not withdraw even when friends become enemies; insofar as it is characterized in all of these ways, God's love serves as a model for the love between human persons. But what serves as *a model* here is precisely God's love for human persons, not human persons' love for God. That is, the way in which we are to love one another is the *way in which God loves us*, not the way in which we are called to love God.

Another way of saying this is that God alone is God. "You shall have no other gods before me" (Exod. 20:3). To love justly is to love God in God's concrete reality as *God* (insofar as we know it and insofar as we are able) and to love human persons in their concrete reality as *human persons* (insofar as we know them and insofar as we are able). Hence, the pattern of human commitments and relationships ought to be a pattern in which each is loved as God loves, not a pattern in which one is loved as God loves and the other is loved as if he or she were God.

Second, the model insofar as it models relationship, and not only love, must be looked at more carefully. It may be that it does not justify but prohibits the exaltation of some humans and the subordination of others. At first glance the relationship between God and human persons at the heart of the Covenant seems, for example, to offer little by way of true mutuality. Equality seems unthinkable, for it is God who gives every gift. Two liberties may meet, two words may be given, but one takes the initiative, and the other responds; God chooses, and the people agree; God commands, and the people are to obey; God sets the terms of the Covenant, and the people accept them.

First glances can be misleading, however. At the center of the Covenant, God says, "I bore you on eagles' wings and brought you to myself" (Exod. 19:4). But the eagle spreads its wings and bears its nestlings on its pinions until they can fly by themselves. In the beginning, then, when the capacity for freedom is barely born in us or scarcely healed from a sickness unto death, God's agency must carry ours. God's freedom and activity are directed toward awakening and empowering our freedom and agency. How else except as free and active shall we participate *as persons* in the Covenant God offers?

One way of reading the Covenant story is to see the terms of the Covenant relationship all set by God (to take the metaphor of the suzerainty treaty as the basis of a complete and definitive interpretation of the structure of the Covenant). But there are other ways of understanding this aspect of the story. For example, God, it is said, sets the terms of the Covenant by giving the Law. The Law, of course, is a gift from God to the people in that it guides the people's loves and sustains a viable community. Yet it is also the people's gift to God. For the Law is a product of the people's life, the means of offering Israel's life to God. Through time laws are interpreted, some of them changed. The people themselves, with the prophets and teachers who they believe are sent by God, discern what Covenant fidelity means, what the "terms" are of enduring love. At the very least, then, it can be said that God shares with the people the task of determining what laws are fundamental to the meaning of love, what new demands evolve as the Covenant relationship grows.

The receiving that is so important in human persons' participation in the Covenant is not, then, always or only passive. As Marcel observed, "to receive" can mean anything from passive undergoing (imprinted upon like wax) to active giving (as when a host "receives" a guest).[27] Hence, it can represent one side of a reality that includes active receptivity and receptive activity. It is possible that both sides of this reality belong to the commitment and the love of both human persons and God.

The possibility of receptivity on God's part is not so difficult to affirm. It can be glimpsed in the life of God's own self as it is interpreted through Christian ponderings of the doctrine of the Trinity. Here is a triune life in which "persons" in God communicate, with mutual and infinitely active receptivity and receptive activity, an utterly shared life that is the life of the Spirit.[28] Insofar as the model for human relationships is not only God's love but the communal form of God's love, it is this pattern of mutuality that serves as a guide. For Christians believe that the pattern of God's relationship with Jesus is the pattern of God's own life, and this ultimately is the pattern offered for relationships between human persons. Once again, "As God has loved me, so have I loved you" (Jn. 15:9) and "even as I have loved you, love one another" (Jn. 13:34).

Still, the Covenant tradition offers a view of God's commitment and God's call to mutuality that approaches the unthinkable. It is a view that finds God breaking even the barriers of ordinary notions of equality. So far does the Covenant story go in pointing to the goal of mutuality that it tells even of God's not fearing to "empty" God's self, to make possible a kind of equality with the persons God creates. Such an understanding of God need not lead believers to "domesticate" God, to trivialize the presence of God as God. Rather, it can be what makes possible a choice of ultimate surrender in absolute love—a surrender that does not contradict the freedom and power of human persons, but brings them to paradoxical completion.

Responsibility in Relation to the World

Finally, there is the question of whether or not a Covenant whose central substance is a relationship can ground hope in and human responsibility for fashioning a better world. This question is closely connected with both the issue of the universality of Covenant love and the issue of the mutuality of the Covenant-relation.

If the presence of God by God's word is only a matter of the mystical presence of God in the world—God in relation to each individual person or God encountered in the sacred places of the community—then there is not much human persons can or need to do. If such is the case, the whole mutuality of the Covenant will be constituted by the knowing and being known, loving and being loved, the communion between God and human persons. Human freedom will be exercised in responding to God's love, holding faithful to the watch for God's presence, waiting for new manifestations of God's glory. Love will be universal in its outreach, warm in its compassion, but limited in its possible deeds. And the major response to human suffering may be alleviating what pain one can, comforting the sorrowful, and trusting in the ultimate healing of God.

The Covenant tradition, however, calls for something more as an adequate interpretation of its meaning. The relationship of the Covenant leans toward the future, not only as sustaining what already is, but as reaching toward what is not yet. Held in its future is the promise of the fullness of union—of universal communion with all human persons and with God. This, however, implies the overcoming of all the barriers that separate human persons and hence the establishment of a realm of justice, the healing of a divided world.

The scope of the promise is the whole of human life. And it does not stop short of death. The mutuality it seeks is love, yes, and trust—but within these, and informing them in the present, is the engagement of hope. The hope it asks for, requires, is not passive, but active. And the scope of its activity matches the scope of the promise. Hence, as Jürgen Moltmann says, *promissio* involves *missio*; if the promise is received, it brings with it a mission.[29] The promise of God that aims toward mutuality includes in its aim the mutuality of mission. The mission is the healing of the world.

The story of the Covenant helps to interpret the hope that the experience of the Covenant awakens. It also provides an agenda for the labors that spring from this hope. A strategic priority, for example, must be given to the most disadvantaged, to those who are outcasts, enslaved, oppressed. The people of the Covenant have always understood this, for were they not themselves favored by God when they were slaves? or called to be disciples with Jesus when they were a people oppressed?

Out of the relationship that is the substance of the Covenant, then, emerges the call and the responsibility to oppose the forces of evil in the world, to nurture the sources of human well-being, to form structures that respect human dignity. Whatever can serve this labor falls within the scope of the Covenant. Always any given labor may end in exile, or in destruction of the land, or in death. Yet the word remains; the relationship holds; hope, and responsibility, can continue.

Not Yet Whole

God's promise is given to persons in via, *while they are not yet capable of perfect fidelity.* There is, then, God's promise and the possibility of human response. In the one lies the hope of the other. Injustice remains and the end of death's domination has only begun. Yet there is hope in a love stronger than death. Intimacy is fragile, human solidarity is more yearned for than celebrated, friends still betray friends, and violence abounds. Yet there is the possibility of a love stronger than the enmity of the beloved. No one knows fulfillment or the end of themselves, and the restless heart still thirsts in this desert of a world. Yet there is a glimpse of a love with inexhaustible life.

The Covenant story is replete with both the promise of glory and the groaning of a creation still in travail. The hope that it grounds is not only for justice and not only for ultimate satisfaction; it is for the possibility of one's own responding love. For this, too, is part of the "already" that is also "not yet." The command is: "Thou shalt, thou canst, love God with all thine heart; and it is given to us to feel that the heart will not become whole except by such a love."[30] In the dimension of time, says Martin Buber, this translates as "Love [God] . . . unto the squeezing out of the soul."[31] But in the mystery of the spontaneity of human love, in the struggle for wholeness in the human heart, the command must include "so far as thou, exerting thyself, art able to do here and now."[32]

Sometimes the ideal of love, whether for God or for human persons, inspires and gives power. Sometimes, however, when its long distance from the capacity of the human heart is most clear, it oppresses and brings despair. Paul's description, for example, of the ideal of love among persons can empower, or it can crush, the human spirit.

> Love is patient and kind; love is not jealous or boastful; it is not arrogant or rude. Love does not insist on its own way; it is not irritable or resentful; it does not rejoice at wrong, but rejoices in the right. Love bears all things, believes all things, hopes all things, endures all things. (1 Cor. 13:4–7)

Those who interpret Paul's words as an absolute expectation experience the hopelessness of their own possibility of response. But for Paul such love is part of a process. It belongs to the future, not only to the present. It is still partial, imperfect, and changing, formed as it is by a vision seen "in a mirror dimly" (13:12). Everything may threaten it and it may be agonizingly incomplete, yet it can survive. It is already actualized, and "love never ends" (13:8); but it has barely begun, so "make love your aim" (14:1).

The incapacities of the human heart may indeed break human hearts, but they need not destroy their loves. The clue to this truth is not outside of but within the meaning of commitment. As we have seen, in lives stretched out in time, there can be no absolute fullness, no utter once and for all yielding of love. Commitment, therefore, is love's way of being whole when it is not yet whole, love's way of offering its incapacities as well as its power. This truth, then, belongs also to the meaning of the Covenant. Here, too, human persons know their own partiality of love. They know their foolishness and their weakness and the inner contradictions that lurk as a threat to their love. Those who bear witness to the Covenant, however, tell of a Promise that will not be revoked, a Love that can hold the incapacities of the beloved. They tell of a Word that abides, and a Spirit that strengthens. They tell of a glory in weakness, and a freedom that is not without power.

These, then, are some of the ways in which the Covenant story provides a context and a ground for all of our commitments to love. It is not the only source of religious wisdom in this regard. It does not even exhaust our ways of knowing the God who covenants. For this God is present with us beyond the lines of the story, in modes of relationship at which the story only hints.

Still, the story of the Covenant, even interpreted with the broad strokes I have used, offers us access to a belief and a hope that can qualify the meaning of every commitment. It manages to speak to the theoretical questions with which I began the first chapter. It may speak also to the questions of concrete persons' lives—like those of Harriet, of Sheila and Joshua, of Henry, and of Stephen and Ann. Insofar as it reveals to us a context in which we may more wisely commit ourselves one to another, it bears witness to the power and courage of human love, the need and hope of human commitments. In and through such commitments as these, it bears witness to a Promise received and a Presence that abides.

Notes

Chapter 1: Commitment and Its Discontents

1. Audre Lorde, *Sister Outsider* (Trumansburg, N.Y.: The Crossing Press, 1984), 119.

2. Kenneth Keniston, *The Uncommitted: Alienated Youth in American Society* (New York: Harcourt, Brace & World, 1960), 186.

3. Margaret Mead, *Culture and Commitment: A Study of the Generation Gap* (Garden City, N.Y.: Doubleday, Natural History Press, 1970), x.

4. Daniel Yankelovich, *New Rules: Search for Self-Fulfillment in a World Turned Upside Down* (New York: Random House, 1981), 250 and *passim*.

5. Robert N. Bellah et al., *Habits of the Heart: Individualism and Commitment in American Life* (Berkeley: University of California Press, 1985), 194 and *passim*.

6. Barbara Ehrenreich, *The Hearts of Men: American Dreams and the Flight from Commitment* (Garden City, N.Y.: Doubleday, Anchor Books, 1984), 182.

7. See, for example, the October 9, 2012, Pew Forum Report on the religious affiliations of Americans. Entitled "'Nones' on the Rise: One-in-Five Adults Have No Religious Affiliation," available online from the Pew Research Center.

8. See as an example the website entitled *LifeScript: Healthy Living for Women*, which provides "5 Reasons You Have Commitment Issues" at LifeScript.com, accessed October 6, 2012.

9. U.S. Census Bureau, Statistical Abstract of the United States: 2012. Accessed October 14, 2012, from *International Statistics*, 840: census.gov/compendia/2012/tables/12s1335. Of some note is the upturn in marriages in Sweden, given its longtime move away from official marriage.

10. This does not mean that others do not focus on these factors in their analysis of the numbers. For an overall historical view in this regard, see Stephanie Coontz, *Marriage, a History: From Obedience to Intimacy or How Love Conquered Marriage* (New York: Viking Penguin, 2005), esp. chap 4. See also Press Release, *Statistics Sweden*, February 18, 2011, accessed October 14, 2012, at scb.se/Pages/PressRelease____308294.aspx; and epp.eurostat.ec.europa.eu/statistics_explained/index.php/Marriage_and_divorce_statistics. In general, it appears that marriage is more likely to be the form of commitment among

the highly educated and economically stable, and couples in these groups are also more likely to stay married than are those with less education and greater economic instability or dire poverty.

11. For further information on these questions, see, e.g., G. Andersson, "Demographic Trends in Sweden: An Update of Childbearing and Nuptiality up to 2002," *Demographic Research* 11: 95–110; J. Surkyn and R. Lesthaeghe, "Value Orientations and the Second Demographic Transition in Northern, Western and Southern Europe: An Update," *Demographic Research Special Collection* 3: 45–86, cited in Sofi Ohlsson, "Trend Reversal in Marriage in Sweden," accessed October 14, 2012, at paa2009.princeton.edu/papers/90232.

12. Robert Jay Lifton, *Boundaries: Psychological Man in Revolution* (New York: Vintage Books, 1970), chap. 4. An earlier theory of social "masks" can be found in Erving Goffman, *The Presentation of Self in Everyday Life* (Garden City, N.Y.: Doubleday, Anchor Books, 1959).

13. Jean-Paul Sartre, *Being and Nothingness*, trans. Hazel E. Barnes (New York: Washington Square Press, 1966), 69.

14. Henry Sidgwick, *The Methods of Ethics* (New York: Dover, 1966), 259.

15. Harry G. Frankfurt, *The Importance of What We Care About: Philosophical Essays* (Cambridge: Cambridge University Press, 1988); Frankfurt, *Taking Ourselves Seriously & Getting It Right*, ed. Debra Satz (Stanford, Calif.: Stanford University Press, 2006), 3 and 5.

16. Charles Taylor, *Sources of the Self: The Making of Modern Identity* (Cam-bridge, Mass: Harvard University Press, 1989). See also Morwenna Griffiths, *Feminisms and the Self: The Web of Identity* (London: Routledge, 1995); Klaus Demmer, *Living the Truth: A Theory of Action*, trans. Brian McNeil (Washington, D.C.: Georgetown University Press, 2010).

17. Agnes Heller, "Death of the Subject," in *Constructions of the Self*, ed. George Levine (New Brunswick, N.J.: Rutgers University Press, 1992), 269–84.

18. Frankfurt, *Taking Ourselves Seriously & Getting It Right*, 51.

19. Paul Ricoeur, *Essays on Biblical Interpretation*, ed. Lewis S. Mudge (Philadelphia: Fortress Press, 1980), 97.

20. I refer here to persons like "Stephen and Ann" more than once throughout this book. They represent "cases" of a sort, without my delineating detailed "case studies." To facilitate following them as they appear in different chapters, their names are included in the index.

Chapter 2: The Meaning of Commitment

1. Not all theorists would describe the meaning of commitment, or of promise-making, in the way I do here. One's definition of a promise is closely tied to one's view of how it obligates. There are at least three

major positions on this that appear in the history of philosophy and in contemporary discussion of promises: (1) the obligation to keep promises is purely conventional—an agreed-upon "practice" or "game" in a given community, sometimes a matter of pretense until it is taken for granted and believed (Hume), sometimes a matter of violent discipline until behavioral conditioning gives it lasting status (Nietzsche); (2) the obligation is produced by the promise itself, for the words of promise are "performative," or "commissive," actually *doing* what they say (Austin, Searle, Melden, Sartre); (3) the obligation to keep promises is ultimately grounded in a more general obligation to respect persons, or to sustain moral community (Aquinas, Kant, Hegel, Hare). Many philosophers hold a combination of these views—for example, asserting that promising produces its own obligation, but only in a context where the conventions are such that this is possible (in other words, the "performative" depends on there being a "practice" of promising). My description of what "happens" when we make a commitment can be understood as a description of commitment as performative, but also (as will be clear in chaps. 6 and 7) assumes a fundamental ground of moral obligation in the reality of persons. Key treatments of these questions include historical works such as David Hume, *A Treatise of Human Nature*, ed. L. A. Selby-Bigge (Oxford: Clarendon Press, 1968), Book III, Part 2, Sec. 5; Georg Hegel, *Philosophy of Right*, trans. T. M. Knox (New York: Oxford University Press, 1967), 57–63; Friedrich Nietzsche, *On a Genealogy of Morals*, trans. W. Kaufmann and R. J. Hollingdale (New York: Vintage Books, 1967), 57–61; linguistic approaches such as J. L. Austin, *How to Do Things with Words*, ed. J. O. Urmson (New York: Oxford University Press, 1962); John R. Searle, *Speech Acts: An Essay in the Philosophy of Language* (Cambridge: University Press, 1970), esp. chaps. 2 and 3; contemporary philosophical discussions such as Pall S. Ardal, "'And That's a Promise,'" and "Reply to New on Promises," *Philosophical Quarterly* 18 and 19 (July 1968 and July 1969); John Rawls, "Two Concepts of Rules," *Philosophical Review* 64 (1955): 3–32; Joseph Raz, "Promises and Obligations," in *Law, Morality and Society: Essays in Honour of H. L. A. Hart*, ed. P. M. S. Hacker and J. Raz (Oxford: Clarendon Press, 1977); G. J. Warnock, *The Object of Morality* (London: Methuen, 1971), chap. 7; and works relevant to contract law, such as Patrick Atiyah, *The Rise and Fall of Freedom of Contract* (Oxford: Clarendon Press, 1979); Charles Fried, *Contract as Promise: A Theory of Contractual Obligation* (Cambridge: Harvard University Press, 1981). A key treatment important for the whole question of promise-making and promise-keeping is the classic study of Josiah Royce on loyalty: *The Philosophy of Loyalty* (New York: Macmillan, 1924).

    2. H. Clay Trumbull, *Blood Covenant: A Primitive Rite and Its Bearings on Scripture* (London: George Redway, 1887), 5 and *passim*.

3. As quoted in Edward Westermarck, *Marriage Ceremonies in Morocco* (London: Macmillan, 1914), 40–41. This same repetition occurs in pre-1965 vow ceremonies in Roman Catholic religious communities. Those making their vows sang "Suscipe me, Domine," repeating it three times.

4. A further discussion of the nature of this obligation, and of what one risks losing, appears in chap. 7.

5. Hannah Arendt, *The Human Condition* (Chicago: University of Chicago Press, 1958), 237.

6. Ibid.

7. Erik Erikson, *Identity, Youth and Crisis* (New York: Norton, 1968), 162.

8. Gabriel Marcel, *Being and Having* (New York: Harper Torchbooks, 1965), 45–46.

Chapter 3: Commitment and Love

1. Annie Dillard, *Pilgrim at Tinker Creek* (New York: Harper's Magazine Press, 1974), 242.

2. Robin Morgan, *The Anatomy of Freedom: Feminism, Physics, and Global Politics* (Garden City, N.Y.: Doubleday Anchor Books, 1982), 155.

3. William Butler Yeats, *Selected Poems and Two Plays of William Butler Yeats*, ed. M. L. Rosenthal (New York: Collier Books, 1962), 145.

4. Carol Gilligan, *In a Different Voice: Psychological Theory and Women's Development* (Cambridge: Harvard University Press, 1982), 67.

5. James Boswell, *Life of Samuel Johnson* (Boston: W. Andrews and L. Blake), 3:13.

6. The following analysis of free choice does not pretend to be complete or to take account of the many possibilities in our experiences of choosing. It goes without saying that a more adequate account must be related to developments in action theory. See, for example, Harry Frankfurt's analysis of the stratification of volition, in "Freedom of the Will and the Concept of a Person," *The Journal of Philosophy* 68 (January 1971).

7. Robert C. Solomon, "Emotions and Choice," in *Explaining Emotions*, ed. Amélie O. Rorty (Berkeley: University of California Press, 1980), 254.

8. Robert C. Solomon, *The Passions: The Myth and Nature of Human Emotion* (Notre Dame: University of Notre Dame Press, 1983), 158.

9. Jules J. Toner, *The Experience of Love* (Washington: Corpus Books, 1968), 65–68.

10. Ibid., 142. My identification of the essential elements in the experience of love as affirmation, union, and response is based on Toner's overall analysis.

11. Graham Greene, *The Power and the Glory* (New York: Penguin Books, 1984), 131.

12. Toner, *The Experience of Love*, 96.

13. Solomon, "Emotions and Choice," 270.

14. Søren Kierkegaard, *Works of Love*, trans. Howard and Edna Hong (New York: Harper Torchbooks, 1962), 45.

15. Jean-Paul Sartre, *Critique of Dialectical Reason*, trans. Alan Sheridan-Smith, ed. Jonathan Ree (London: NLB, 1978), 431.

16. Søren Kierkegaard, *Either/Or*, II, trans. W. Lowrie (Garden City, N.Y.: Doubleday, Anchor Books, 1958), 149.

17. By use of the term "worthiness" here I do not imply that some persons, as persons, are unworthy of our commitment to love. I do imply, however, that on the basis of different realities, some commitments are justified in relation to God, some in relation to human persons, and that the individual reality of a human person is relevant to considerations of the appropriateness of certain commitments. This will become clearer, I believe, in my treatment of "just love" in chap. 7.

18. W. David Ross, *Foundations of Ethics* (Oxford: Clarendon Press, 1939), 99.

Chapter 4: The Way of Fidelity

1. Henri Bergson, *Creative Evolution,* trans. A. Mitchell (New York: Holt, 1911), 340. For the general notion of the "between," I am indebted to Bergson's other works as well, especially *The Creative Mind*, trans. M. L. Andison (Totowa, N.J.: Littlefield, Adams, and Co., 1965), and *Time and Free Will: An Essay on the Immediate Data of Consciousness*, trans. F. L. Pogson (New York: Macmillan, 1959).

2. Maurice Merleau-Ponty, *Phenomenology of Perception*, trans. Colin Smith (New York: Humanities Press, 1967), 416. Merleau-Ponty is heavily dependent for his analysis of time on the earlier work of Edmund Husserl, *The Phenomenology of Internal Time-Consciousness*, ed. M. Heidegger, trans. J. S. Churchill (Bloomington: Indiana University Press, 1969), esp. 40–57. My analysis is indebted to both Husserl and Merleau-Ponty.

3. The process philosopher Alfred North Whitehead argued that at every level of being, process cannot exist without decision, without the cutting off of some possibilities for the sake of actualizing others. See, for example, *Process and Reality* (New York: Macmillan, 1929), 68; *Modes of Thought* (New York: Free Press, 1968), 152.

4. Gabriel Marcel, *Creative Fidelity*, trans. Robert Rosthal (New York: Noonday Press, 1964), 153.

5. Ibid., 155.

6. Charles Williams's primary work on a theology of romantic love appears in his *The Figure of Beatrice in Dante* (New York: Noonday Press, 1961). A very helpful study of this theme in all of his works is provided by Mary McDermott

Shideler's *The Theology of Romantic Love: A Study in the Writings of Charles Williams* (Grand Rapids: Eerdmans, 1962).

7. See Shideler, *The Theology of Romantic Love: A Study in the Writings of Charles Williams*, 115.

8. Williams, *The Figure of Beatrice in Dante*, 35.

9. An important caveat should be entered here in the case of serious abuse or violence (physical or emotional) perpetrated against one of the partners in a commitment relationship. It can, in such instances, be quite clear that the "original vision" was mistaken, or that it has been contradicted in time.

10. This term is Ursula Niebuhr's. I was first introduced to it in Christopher F. Mooney's *Man without Tears: Soundings for a Christian Anthropology* (New York: Harper & Row, 1975), 75.

Chapter 5: Conditions for Presence

1. This is a significantly different approach to fidelity and perseverance from the one pursued by, for example, Rosabeth Moss Kanter in her studies of commitment in utopian communities. While the factors that Kanter identifies (continuance, cohesion, and control) are extremely illuminating regarding strategies of perseverance, they focus on social control of the human will in a way that does not appear to take account of the capacity (and need) in human persons for continual expansion of mind and heart. The other categories that Kanter names (sacrifice/investment, renunciation/communion, and mortification/surrender) represent formidable restrictions (rather than nurturants) of vision and love. Insofar as this is the case, "presence" may be achieved, but it is not a fully human one. I am not sure whether the problem here is with the subject of Kanter's study or with the method of analysis. The aim of the study is, of course, completely different from this one. I interpret the two kinds of study as importantly complementary. See Rosabeth Moss Kanter, "Commitment and Social Organization: A Study of Commitment Mechanisms in Utopian Communities," *American Sociological Review* 33 (August, 1968): 499–517; and Kanter, *Commitment and Community: Communes and Utopias in Sociological Perspective* (Cambridge: Harvard University Press, 1972). My approach to fidelity in this chapter is also significantly different from those writers (from the Greek philosophers onward) whose major concern is with "weakness of will" or "backsliding," or (especially) "viciousness." To some extent these considerations appear in chaps. 6 and 7 in my treatment of obligation. Helpful studies in this regard include Mary Midgley, *Wickedness: A Philosophical Essay* (London: Routledge & Kegan Paul, 1984), esp. 58–61; David Wiggins, "Weakness of Will, Commensurability, and the Objects of Deliberation and Desire," in *Essays on Aristotle's Ethics*, ed. Amelie Oksenberg Rorty (Berkeley: University of California Press, 1980), 241–65; Donald

Davidson, "How Is Weakness of the Will Possible?," in *Moral Concepts*, ed. J. Feinberg (New York: Oxford University Press, 1969), 93–113; and Bernard A. O. Williams, "Ethical Consistency," in *Problems of the Self* (London: Cambridge University Press, 1972), 166–86.

2. Alice Walker, *Meridian* (New York: Washington Square Press, 1976), 200–201.

3. Gerard Manley Hopkins, "God's Grandeur," in *The Poems of Gerard Manley Hopkins*, ed. W. H. Gardner and N. H. MacKenzie, 4th rev. ed. (New York: Oxford University Press, 1970), 66.

4. Annie Dillard, *Teaching a Stone to Talk: Expeditions and Encounters* (New York: Harper & Row, 1982), 76.

5. Emily Dickinson, *The Poems of Emily Dickinson*, vol. 2, ed. Thomas J. Johnson (Cambridge: Belknap Press of Harvard University Press, 1955), Poem #997, 721.

6. Barbara Ehrenreich, *The Hearts of Men: American Dreams and the Flight from Commitment* (Garden City, N.Y.: Doubleday, Anchor Books, 1984), 96.

7. Gabriel Marcel, *Homo Viator*, trans. Emma Craufurd (New York: Harper Torchbooks, 1962), 39.

8. Etty Hillesum, *An Interrupted Life: The Diaries of Etty Hillesum 1941–1943*, trans. Arnold J. Pomerans (New York: Pantheon Books, 1983), 75.

9. Rainer Maria Rilke, *Sonnets to Orpheus*, I, 4, trans. M. D. Herter Norton (New York: Norton, 1942), 23.

10. Lillian Breslow Rubin, *Worlds of Pain: Life in the Working-Class Family* (New York: Basic Books, 1976), 120–21.

11. Sigrid Undset, *Kristin Lavransdatter*, trans. Charles Archer and J. S. Scott (New York: Bantam Books, 1978), 2:14, 15, 24.

12. Laurence Kubie as quoted in Jessie Bernard, *The Future of Marriage,* rev. ed. (New Haven: Yale University Press, 1982), 118.

13. Margaret R. Miles, "The Courage to Be Alone—In and Out of Marriage," in *The Feminist Mystic: and Other Essays on Women and Spirituality*, ed. Mary E. Giles (New York: Crossroad, 1982), 96.

14. Ehrenreich, *The Hearts of Men*, 182.

Chapter 6: Discerning Obligation: Can There Be Release?

1. Howard S. Becker, "Notes on the Concept of Commitment," *American Journal of Sociology* 66 (July 1960): 32–40.

2. See description of what it means to make a commitment in chap. 2. When promising is considered as self-obligating, it is sometimes called a "performative"—a use of words, or some other form of communication, that actually effects a new state of affairs, a new form of relationship. For one version of this, see A. I. Melden, *Rights and Persons* (Berkeley: University of California

180   *Personal Commitments*

Press, 1980), esp. chap. 2. For a discussion of this in the context of debates about obligation in Christian ethics, see Donald Evans, "Love, Situations, and Rules," in *Norm and Context in Christian Ethics*, ed. Gene H. Outka and Paul Ramsey (New York: Scribner, 1968), 367–414. The relevant linguistic theories are in J. L. Austin, *How to Do Things with Words*, ed. J. O. Urmson (New York: Oxford University Press, 1962), and John R. Searle, *Speech Acts: An Essay in the Philosophy of Language* (Cambridge: Cambridge University Press, 1970).

3. For a view of promise-keeping that takes account of consequences as well as the self-obligating aspect of the promise, see W. D. Ross, *Foundations of Ethics*, esp. 53–56, 89–113; Evans, "Love, Situations, and Rules"; R. M. Hare, *Freedom and Reason* (New York: Oxford University Press, 1965), 130–36. For a wholly utilitarian view of promise-keeping, see W. A. Pickard-Cambridge, "Two Problems about Duty," *Mind* 41 (1932): 72–96, 145–72, 311–40.

4. Cicero, *De Officiis,* Loeb Classical Library, vol. 21 (Cambridge: Harvard University Press, 1968), I: 32, 30–40; III: 92–95. It should be noted here that though I am focusing on Western traditions, it is typical of most other civilizations both to honor ordinary obligations entailed in promise-keeping and commitment-making as necessary for societal survival, but to limit them as well.

5. Thomas Aquinas, *Summa Theologiae II–II*, 88, loc; 89, 7. Interestingly, while Aquinas sees commitment as self-obligation ("The obligation of a vow proceeds from the will" [II–II, 189, 4]), vows that cannot be dispensed (that can never be released) have this binding character not because they are made as perpetual vows but because, argues Thomas, they "consecrate" a person (in the same way that a chalice is consecrated), and no one can take that reality away (*ST* II–II, 88, 10 ad 1; 88, 1lc).

6. Immanuel Kant, *Fundamental Principles of the Metaphysic of Morals*, trans. Thomas K. Abbott (New York: Library of Liberal Arts, 1949), 39–40.

7. Immanuel Kant, *Lectures on Ethics* (New York: Harper Torchbooks, 1963), 208.

8. Immanuel Kant, *The Metaphysical Elements of Justice*, trans. John Ladd (New York: Library of Liberal Arts, 1965), 40; see also *The Metaphysical Principles of Virtue*, trans. James Ellington (New York: Library of Liberal Arts, 1964), 19.

9. Richard A. McCormick, *Notes on Moral Theology 1965 through 1980* (Washington: University Press of America, 1981), 709.

10. Paul Ramsey, "The Case of the Curious Exception," in *Norm and Context in Christian Ethics*, ed. G. Outka and P. Ramsey, 67–135. It should be noted that Ramsey's position rules out release from significant commitments and would be in direct disagreement with the general approach of McCormick.

11. Melden, *Rights and Persons*, 4.

12. G. E. M. Anscombe, "On Promising and Its Justice, and Whether It

Need be Respected in *Foro Interno*," in *Ethics, Religion and Politics,* Collected
Philosophical Papers (Minneapolis: University of Minnesota Press, 1981), 3:15.

13. Thomas Aquinas, *Summa Theologiae* II–II, 88, 2 ad 3.

14. See my discussion of limits at the end of chap. 2.

15. I am well aware that this is not a limiting condition included explicitly in
traditional marriages. Growing reflectiveness on the phenomenon of battering
(or spouse abuse), however, makes prohibition of this a likely candidate for an
implicit but essential condition for the marriage.

16. Charles Fried, *Contract as Promise: A Theory of Contractual Obligation*
(Cambridge: Harvard University Press, 1981), 58.

17. Melden, *Rights and Persons*, 150.

18. Graham Greene, *The Heart of the Matter* (New York: Penguin Books,
1982), 161-62.

19. Søren Kierkegaard, *Works of Love*, trans. Howard and Edna Hong (New
York: Harper Torchbooks, 1964), 184.

20. See treatment of this regarding friendship in Gilbert C. Meilaender,
Friendship: A Study in Theological Ethics (Notre Dame: University of Notre
Dame Press, 1981), esp. chap. 3.

21. Thomas Aquinas, *Summa Theologiae* II–II, 88, 3 ad 2.

22. Augustine, *Ep.* 139, 3 to Marcellinus, as quoted in Marie Aquinas
McNamara, *Friendship in Saint Augustine* (Fribourg: University Press, 1958), 222.

Chapter 7: Discerning Obligation: A Just Love

1. My approach to a standard for a right love is influenced by Jules Toner's
discussion of truth and falsity in love. See *The Experience of Love* (Washington:
Corpus Books, 1968), 156–62. My reasons for preferring the term "just love"
should be clear in the context of my own discussion. See also Margaret A.
Farley, *Just Love: A Framework for Christian Sexual Ethics* (New York: Continuum
International, 2006).

2. An obvious example is women's objections through the centuries to
being stereotyped in ways that seem to deny their own experience and self-
understanding as women.

3. How we interpret this complex structure will make a great deal of
difference in what we affirm for human persons. For example, if we think that
emotions are the primary element in the human personality, we will have a
different view of personal well-being than if we think that rationality is primary.
Or if in our view freedom is of central importance to the human person, we
will affirm quite different things than if we think a person's place in an organic
society is of such value that freedom should be negligible. My purpose here
is not to settle all the questions of interpretation regarding human reality; it is
only to insist that concern for a just love points us to (among other things) the
task of such interpretation.

4. See description of love in chap. 3.

5. The question of responsibility for our own incapacities is an extremely complex question that I cannot treat adequately in this book. I refer to it later in the chapter, but again only in passing. I mean to suggest the difficulty of the question by alluding to doctrines of original sin as well as to our own obvious choices that have consequences in making fidelity impossible for us. But I leave a full discussion of these matters to another study.

6. R. M. Hare, *Freedom and Reason* (New York: Oxford University Press, 1965), 59–60.

7. For a distinction between "psychological" and "physical" impossibility, see Hare, *Freedom and Reason*, 80–82. See also Richard A. McCormick, *Notes on Moral Theology 1965 through 1980* (Washington: University Press of America, 1981), 142–43; and for a classical distinction in moral theology between "absolute" and "moral" impossibility, see, for example, Dominic M. Prummer, *Handbook of Moral Theology*, trans. G. W. Shelton (New York: P. J. Kenedy & Sons, 1957), 46–47, 226–27.

8. Theodore Mackin, *Divorce and Remarriage* (New York: Paulist Press, 1984), 507.

9. Jessie Bernard, *The Future of Marriage*, rev. ed. (New Haven: Yale University Press, 1982), x.

10. Sigrid Undset, *Kristin Lavransdatter*, trans. Charles Archer & J. S. Scott (New York: Bantam Books, 1978), 2: 312 (my italics).

11. Bernard, *The Future of Marriage*, 281.

12. Ibid.

13. Theodore Mackin, *What Is Marriage?* (New York: Paulist Press, 1982), 344–45. This is the view of marriage as a juridical relation that Mackin attributes to a part (though by no means all) of the Roman Catholic tradition—and here, specifically, to Pope Paul VI. I do not treat the very complex issues that are particular to this tradition, though my intention is not thereby to dismiss them as unimportant. The problems of release from marital commitments (for divorce and, then, remarriage) in Roman Catholicism indeed deserve careful and sometimes highly technical analysis and evaluation. Mackin's two-volume work on the subject offers an excellent treatment of historical and contemporary developments in this regard.

14. Bernard, *The Future of Marriage*, 271–72.

15. Dorothy Day, *By Little and By Little: The Selected Writings of Dorothy Day*, ed. Robert Ellsberg (New York: Knopf, 1983), 39.

16. Ibid., 37–38.

17. Stuart Hampshire, "Public and Private Morality," in Stuart Hampshire et al., *Public and Private Morality* (Cambridge: Cambridge University Press, 1978), 46.

18. Henrik Ibsen, *A Doll's House,* Act III, in *Four Major Plays,* trans. Rolf Fjelde (New York: New American Library, 1965),1:110–11.

19. A treatment of these issues that remains of major importance is to be found in Gene Outka, *Agape: An Ethical Analysis* (New Haven: Yale University Press, 1972), esp. chaps. 2 and 8. See also Gilbert C. Meilaender, *Friendship: A Study in Theology Ethics* (Notre Dame: University of Notre Dame Press, 1981), chap. 2. For important developments in feminist thinking on the subject of self-sacrifice, mutuality, and moral development, see Carol Gilligan, *In a Different Voice: Psychological Theory and Women's Development* (Cambridge: Harvard University Press, 1982); see also Christine E. Gudorf, "Parenting, Mutual Love, and Sacrifice," in *Women's Consciousness, Women's Conscience: A Reader in Feminist Ethics,* ed. Barbara Hilkert Andolsen, Christine E. Gudorf, and Mary D. Pellauer (Minneapolis: Winston Press, 1985), 175–91.

20. Karl Rahner, *Dangers dans le catholicisme d'aujourd'hui,* French trans. R. Givord (Paris: Desclée de Brouwer, 1958), 87, as quoted in Cahal B. Daly, "Natural Law Morality Today," *The American Ecclesiastical Review* 153 (December 1965): 389.

21. Alan Paton, *Ah, But Your Land Is Beautiful* (New York: Penguin Books, 1981), 23–24.

22. Thomas Aquinas, *Summa Theologiae* II–II, 26, 6.

23. See, for example, the principle delineated for determining responsibility to prevent and correct social injury in John G. Simon, Charles Powers, and Jon P. Gunnemann, *The Ethical Investor: Universities and Corporate Responsibility* (New Haven: Yale University Press, 1972), 22–25.

24. See the helpful treatment of conflict of values in the Roman Catholic tradition in David Hollenbach, *Claims in Conflict: Retrieving and Renewing the Catholic Human Rights Tradition* (New York: Paulist Press, 1979), esp. chaps. 4 and 5.

Chapter 8: Commitment, Covenant, and Faith

1. D. J. McCarthy, *Old Testament Covenant: A Survey of Current Opinions* (Richmond, Va.: John Knox Press, 1972), 1. A helpful study of the covenant from the standpoint of commitment and loyalty can be found in Katharine Doob Sakenfeld, *Faithfulness in Action: Loyalty in Biblical Perspective* (Philadelphia: Fortress Press, 1985). See also Delbert R. Hillers, *Covenant: The History of a Biblical Idea* (Baltimore: Johns Hopkins University Press, 1969).

2. See Donald D. Evans, *The Logic of Self-Involvement* (New York: Herder and Herder, 1969). Evans argues that the biblical conception of creation includes the notion of God's self-commitment. See esp. 157–60. See also Gerhard von Rad, *Old Testament Theology,* vol. I: *The Theology of Israel's Historical Traditions,* trans. D. M. G. Stalker (New York: Harper and Row, 1962), 139–53;

Walther Eichrodt, *Theology of the Old Testament*, trans. J. A. Baker (Philadelphia: Westminster Press, 1961), esp. 1:49–51, 56–58. There is, of course, a serious controversy among biblical scholars as to whether or not the concept of Covenant was simply read back into the early texts, retrojecting a tradition that began only with the Sinaitic covenant. More recently, efforts have been made to show that the Covenant theme is not as all-pervasive as some scholars have previously thought. My own use of the theme does not finally depend on the resolution of either of these questions, for I am not arguing that Covenant is the single most important biblical theme; and the theological implications of Covenant for interpreting God's creative actions do not require that the earliest biblical authors intended to explicate the concept of Covenant.

3. Nils Alstrup Dahl, *Studies in Paul: Theology for the Early Christian Mission* (Minneapolis: Augsburg, 1977), 123. Dahl goes on to add: "One would go too far to claim that Paul always maintains the distinction between confirmation of promise and the more general idea that events happen according to the Scriptures." He notes, however, that only Acts 13:33 uses the expression that God has "fulfilled" God's promise (see 121).

4. Ibid., chap. 1, p. 17.

5. Phyllis Trible, *God and the Rhetoric of Sexuality* (Philadelphia: Fortress Press, 1978), 1–5. See also Sakenfeld, *Faithfulness in Action*, 43–76.

6. There is obviously a danger in seeming to collapse the Jewish and Christian notions of the Covenant into one. I am, however, taking the position that there is continuity between the two. As Elisabeth Schüssler Fiorenza points out, the Jesus movement was a movement within Judaism. And while later developments in Christianity marked a break from Judaism, efforts were made to find continuity in the notion of the Covenant (not always efforts in a form that either Schüssler Fiorenza or I would agree with). See *In Memory of Her: A Feminist Theological Reconstruction of Christian Origins* (New York: Crossroad, 1983), esp. chap. 4.

7. See ibid., 82.

8. See Phyllis Trible, *Texts of Terror: Literary-Feminist Readings of Biblical Narratives* (Philadelphia: Fortress Press, 1984), and James L. Crenshaw, *A Whirlpool of Torment: Israelite Traditions of God as an Oppressive Presence* (Philadelphia: Fortress Press, 1984).

9. Crenshaw, *A Whirlpool of Torment*, ix.

10. This passage appears in Pierre Teilhard de Chardin, "How I Believe," in *Christianity and Evolution*, trans. Rene Hague (New York: Harcourt Brace Jovanovich, 1971), 131. I have, however, used the translation given by Christopher F. Mooney, in *Teilhard de Chardin and the Mystery of Christ* (New York: Harper & Row, 166), 144.

11. See Teilhard de Chardin, *Christianity and Evolution*, chap. 4.

12. Ronald M. Green, *Religious Reason: The Rational and Moral Basis of Religious Belief* (New York: Oxford University Press, 1978), 127.

13. Ibid., 128. Green's case is somewhat weakened by the exceptions noted on 129, n. 7.

14. Teilhard de Chardin, "How I Believe," 132; Mooney translation of *Teilhard de Chardin and the Mystery of Christ*, 145.

15. See Sakenfeld, *Faithfulness in Action*, 64ff.

16. There is, of course, the further problem of why God even *allows* such evil. It is simply not possible here, however, to take on all the issues of theodicy.

17. Crenshaw, *A Whirlpool of Torment*, 115.

18. See ibid., 36–37, 90, 98–99, 102.

19. See Dahl, *Studies in Paul*, esp. 127–36, 170–76.

20. See Hans Joachim Schoeps, "Paul's Misunderstanding of the Law," in *The Writings of St. Paul*, ed. Wayne A. Meeks (New York: W. W. Norton & Company, Inc., 1972), 357.

21. See Martin Buber, *Two Types of Faith: A Study of the Interpenetration of Judaism and Christianity*, trans. Norman P. Goldhawk (New York: Harper Torchbooks, 1961), 93.

22. The comparisons are primarily with Hittite treaties. The historical connection between the Sinai formula and these treaties is debated, but there are nonetheless strong parallels to be noted. See Klaus Baltzer, *The Covenant Formulary: In Old Testament, Jewish, and Early Christian Writings*, trans. David E. Green (Philadelphia: Fortress Press, 1971). See also McCarthy, *Old Testament Covenant*, 10–34; von Rad, *Old Testament Theology*, 1: 129–35.

23. The whole Sinai pericope in Exodus 19–34 is, as Baltzer says, fraught with textual difficulties (which is why Baltzer chooses Joshua 24 as the primary example of treaty formulary influence). Nonetheless, there is no reason not to take account at least of the Exodus 19:3–8 passage, a text that Baltzer observes is "*in nuce* . . . already a complete covenant ceremony" (Baltzer, *The Covenant Formulary*, 29).

24. Green, *Religious Reason*, 136.

25. Dahl cites all of these reasons from the rabbinic tradition in *Studies in Paul,* chap. 10. See also Green, *Religious Reason*, 160–61.

26. See Sakenfeld, *Faithfulness in Action*, 42–43.

27. Gabriel Marcel, *Creative Fidelity*, trans. Robert Rosthal (New York: Noonday Press, 1964), 89–91; also Marcel, *The Philosophy of Existentialism*, trans. Manya Harari (New York: Citadel Press, 1964), 98–101; and Marcel, *Being and Having: An Existential Diary* (New York: Harper Torchmark, 1961), 69, 212.

28. For a fuller treatment of this interpretation of Trinitarian life, see Margaret A. Farley, "New Patterns of Relationship: Beginnings of A Moral Revolution," *Theological Studies* 36 (December 1975), esp. 640–43.

29. Jürgen Moltmann, *The Theology of Hope: On the Ground and the Implications of a Christian Eschatology*, trans. James W. Leitch (New York: Harper & Row, 1967), 225.

30. Buber, *Two Types of Faith*, 136.

31. Ibid.

32. Ibid., 79.

Index